Charles Augustin Sainte-Beuve, Helen G Scott

Portraits of Women

Charles Augustin Sainte-Beuve, Helen G Scott

Portraits of Women

ISBN/EAN: 9783744723893

Printed in Europe, USA, Canada, Australia, Japan

Cover: Foto ©ninafisch / pixelio.de

More available books at **www.hansebooks.com**

PORTRAITS OF WOMEN

BY C. A. SAINTE-BEUVE

TRANSLATED BY

HELEN STOTT

CHICAGO
A. C. M'CLURG, & CO.
1891

CONTENTS.

	PAGE
PREFATORY NOTE,	vii
MADAME DE MAINTENON, 1851,	1
MADAME DE SÉVIGNÉ, 1829,	22
MADAME DE STAËL, 1835,	43
JEANNE D'ARC, 1850,	134
MARIE ANTOINETTE, 1851,	153
MADAME DE LA FAYETTE, 1836,	170

PREFATORY NOTE.

In compiling this volume of Sainte-Beuve's studies of illustrious women, I have not confined my choice to his "Portrait" studies, but have selected from them and from his *Causeries* the essays which appeared to me most likely not only to interest English readers, but also those which exemplify the exploring and far-reaching erudition which the great French critic has brought to bear upon the complex science of literary criticism. His method is original; his style, neither very ponderous nor very brilliant, is essentially penetrating and analytic. He read and studied, carefully observed and noted, every natural trait in a writer as an individual; every literary characteristic; recognised every shade of opinion, discussed these opinions liberally; and then, with infinite subtlety of understanding and great copiousness of language, he boldly clothed his subject with his own convictions, making, as he himself has said, his "praise prominent and his criticism unobtrusive," blending enchantment with his smiling sarcasm, fascinating ever and anon by those flashes of poetic prose which relieve some of his most curiously-enveloped passages.

In another volume of this series there is a critical memoir of Sainte-Beuve by Mr. William Sharp, and to that it is unnecessary to add in this volume. I quote, however, one or two passages from the Reminiscences of his latest secretary, M. Jules Troubat, which disclose in an interesting and graphic manner the private life of the celebrated critic :—

"On the day my duties began, I was conducted by a narrow carpeted staircase to the master's study. Sainte-Beuve just touched my hand without grasping it, holding his fingers straight, after the priestly fashion. At one corner of the table was a little silver saucepan with the remains of milk in it. He had just finished his frugal luncheon, which consisted of tea with milk and two rolls spread with fresh butter,—an English fashion, or one acquired at Boulogne in his childhood. He always left a little of this bread and milk, and put it in a corner by the fireside for Mignonne.* This was how he kept his head clear and cool for work; his feet he kept warm in winter by the aid of a foot-warmer, which was also placed in the carriage on Thursdays when he went to the Academy. He took the greatest care of his brain, using nothing to excite it, not even coffee, and never smoking; the utmost stimulant he ever allowed himself was the 'About' mixture, a little Curaçoa with a suspicion of rum, for which the witty author of the *Roi des Montagnes* had given him the recipe. Dinner, more substantial than luncheon, was delicately composed of soup, roast meat of some kind, salad, vegetables, cheese, fruit, or cake,—a special kind of cake, which was got from the baker in the Rue Fleurus. He had a weakness for strawberries, and sometimes ate

---

* This little cat *Mignonne* deserves a word. When she died, she was greatly regretted by the master. She was the only cat he ever tolerated in his study ; he even allowed her little velvet paws to wander about with daring familiarity among the books and papers which covered his two tables. She had soft, sweet eyes, which lighted lovingly at a caressing touch, with an almost speaking expression in them.

them with sugar at night before retiring to rest. He took scarcely a saucerful of *chocolat au lait* in the morning, and no bread.

"He believed himself that his five years' engagement with the *Constitutionnel* obliged him to diet himself thus carefully, in order to regulate his talent and intellect. Each article he wrote was worth a hundred crowns to him. His patrimony was small; from his mother he had inherited the house he lived in, with an income of about two thousand *livres*.

"He made me a sign to sit down on the easy-chair between the bed and the fireplace, an easy-chair in green repp, historic in its simplicity, and in which all Sainte-Beuve's visitors had sat.

"'There,' he said, pointing to a pile of fifteen volumes, 'are Veuillot's articles; I have to write on him this week, so all that has to be swallowed. Monday, Tuesday, Wednesday, and Thursday, I dictate the article which will appear on the following Monday, read, take notes, and think over the next article; Friday I put that on paper, a labour . . . painful too ; . . . Saturday and Sunday we correct the proofs of Monday's article. . . . Therefore my bad temper begins on Monday ; Tuesday it is worse; Wednesday at its height; Thursday quite as bad ; Friday I am invisible all day, at home to no one ; I put cotton in my ears so that no external sound will jar upon me : I *build* up my article as a tailor *builds* a coat. . . .'

"And, indeed, the rough drafts or jottings which issued from his hands on the Friday evenings when he had *built* the article (as he said), composed of scraps pinned together, very much resembled the first lining of a costume ready for fitting on.

"'My good temper,' he continued, 'does not return till the Sunday evening at six o'clock, when the last pull of proofs for the *Constitutionnel* has been corrected and signed. . . . I then feel relieved, set free. . . . I have a few hours before me. . . . I give you a holiday on Sunday afternoon, but for myself I never have one. . . . I have no Sunday . . . all days are alike in nature.

"'We live without any ceremony; when you come in the evening, if you find me still at table with Mme. Dufour, you must just sit down and join in the conversation. There will be no restraint, and therefore you must pay no attention to my bad times. You can understand, when one feels bound for five years to do the same work each week—and each day—one must have occasional fits of impatience. . . . My life is like a mill, a perpetual feeding and grinding. . . . Cheron at the Library tells me I shall overdo it some day. Thursdays I have the Academy, but I do not go there always: I have quarrelled several times with my colleagues there. They are insignificant people. What can I do? I get there with my head already excited by my work, and I fight with them.'

"At this I laughed,—I could not help it,—and he laughed with me.

"Much has been said of Sainte-Beuve's ill-favoured appearance, a prejudice which still prevails. For my part, I think that ugliness or beauty is conditional. We must consult men as regards beauty in women, and ask a woman's opinion as to whether a man is handsome or not. Sainte-Beuve had a very expressive face, illuminated with the light which intellectual, high-purposed work alone gives.

"He was not one of those who believe that the name is sufficient in literature. He was for ever spurring himself on, as if he had to be continually whetting his talent. Of short stature, straight and portly; his full face closely shaved each day; a large nose ('an inquisitive nose,' as Eugène Pelletan said, speaking of Napoleon III.), one of those inquiring, prying noses, so to speak; the bald outline of his head showed the point of a philosopher's cranium, — 'a sage after the fashion of the ancient Greeks, to whom externally he bore no slight resemblance,'—his bushy reddish eyebrows overhung his eyes, roofed them in; and the legendary velvet cap moved lightly with quick-coming thoughts, or twisted and turned about in his hand in expressing some metaphorical meaning, just as the advocates use their flat-crowned caps in heated argument.

"The study was furnished with a simplicity which a Goncourt would not understand in a man (especially a man living in his own thoughts) like Sainte-Beuve. A bed by the side of the door, two tables joined together in the middle of the room, no ornaments, nor any artistic object except the bust—or rather a miniature of the bust—by Mathieu-Meusnier, which gives such a noble and moreover a real idea of the countenance of the great master, and of which the original makes the pendant to that of Daunou in the Library of Boulogne-sur-Mer, his native town."

This is Troubat's portrait of the celebrated literary critic, whose works, so highly esteemed in France, are increasingly read in England. From this glimpse of the man and of his method, we are able to form an idea of the minute and painstaking research he brought to bear upon the studies he so voluminously produced. In the essays on seven celebrated women which compose this volume, we find a chivalrous delicacy of style, and a scrupulous appreciation of the sacredness of literary effort, which softens the pungency of critical judgment. There is a varied expressiveness, also, in his choice of words, which makes his prose poetic; and we remark, that while the distinct vein of poetry in his nature never disturbs the philosophical subtlety with which he renders each study a complete and scientific analysis, it yet lends real charm to the language in which he clothes his judgments which not even the ordeal of translation can quite destroy.

H S.

March 1891.

MADAME DE MAINTENON.

1851.

THE present seems a favourable time in which to approach the subject of Mme. de Maintenon. Popular taste inclines to display a keen interest in matters which relate to that great century when Louis XIV. reigned ; and as soon as we begin to consider that epoch intellectually, it becomes evident that she must occupy in it a very prominent place. Mme. de Maintenon's mental qualifications cause us to pardon her all those errors with which history justly reproaches her. Her faults were greatly exaggerated at the time by the general public. Mme. de Maintenon did not in reality originate any of the great political acts of the time. Except in one or two instances, which, however, are quite open to dispute, she did no more than favour very zealously the wrongs which were perpetrated during that closing reign. Her chief concern seems to have been to find interesting and amusing occupations, within his necessarily restricted circle, for the latter years of Louis XIV. This is the attitude, indeed the sole part she assumes in her language, her conversation, and also her correspondence, which certainly proves this clearly the more carefully it is studied. She is one of those persons we may hastily condemn, but who, on closer criticism, cannot be so misjudged. She commands respect by her tone of noble simplicity and dignified discretion; she pleases by the piquancy and excellence of her reasoning. There are even moments when we would call her charming; although we no sooner find ourselves beyond her spell than the charm is broken, and we resume our former prejudice against her. I do not know if I am expressing the sentiments of others, but this is my own feeling each time that I approach the subject of Mme. de Maintenon. I shall endeavour to make out a few of my reasons, and to explain them.

Mme. de Maintenon has of late years found a very desirable historian in one of her own kinsmen, M. le Duc de Noailles, who writes most gravely and delicately. The last half of his History is anxiously looked for; I shall make ample use of the two volumes already published, allowing myself, however, a little more freedom or licence in my judgment.

Born in 1635, in the conciergerie of the prison of Niort, where her father was for the time confined, Françoise d'Aubigné began life as in a romance, and, indeed, the strangest romance which could have happened to a person who above all her other characteristics was sensible. A grand-daughter of the illustrious Captain d'Aubigné, who distinguished himself in the sixteenth century, the daughter of the profligate Count Constant d'Aubigné and of a wise, good mother, she had early experience of the strangeness and harshness of fate; yet her heart held a drop of the noble blood of her ancestor, which gave her pride, and she would not have changed her condition for a more fortunate one of lower degree. As a child she accompanied her parents to Martinique. On her return, being under the care of a Huguenot aunt, she had, although born a Catholic, embraced the doctrines of Calvin, when another relation, Mme. de Neuillant, came with an order from the court to rescue her from heresy. Placed first in a convent at Niort, then removed to Paris, the young D'Aubigné, now altogether orphaned, felt every moment of her life the bitterness of dependence. Mme. de Neuillant, so zealous for her spiritual welfare, was so miserably mean that she allowed her to want for everything. However, the young girl began in her visits to Paris to see the world, and from the first she made a successful appearance there. "That was the epoch of elevated conversation, of gallant compliments; in a word, of what was called the *ruelles.*" Wit easily attained a position which was almost honour. *La jeune Indienne,* as she was called on account of her sojourn in America, was remarkable even at first sight, and she lost nothing on closer acquaintance. The Chevalier de Méré, a fashionable wit of the time, became her lover and instructor, and proclaimed her praises. He has described her at this time as possessing a calm and even temper, "very handsome, with a kind of beauty which always pleased." He recommended her to the Duchesse de Lesdiguières, who travelled much, as one who had many charming resources. "She is sweet, grateful, trustworthy, faithful, modest, intelligent, and, to crown her charms, she *uses her wit only to amuse or to make herself beloved.*" When Mlle. d'Aubigné, on her return to Poitou, wrote to her young friends in Paris, her letters were passed round as *chefs-d'œuvre,* and kept up her growing reputation. It was about this time she came to know Scarron, the cripple, a man of gay humour, which passed at that time for delicate wit. Surrounded by affectation, Scarron, with his merry, comical style, was as an antidote. He saw Mlle. d'Aubigné, and, to his credit, was at once interested in her. After some reflection, he thought that the simplest way of testifying this interest, and of aiding her, was to marry her. She consented, giving naïvely enough her reason: "I prefer to marry him rather than become a nun." She has never mentioned her *poor cripple* but with suitable respect and esteem, as a man of integrity, and of a much more kindly disposition than those who judged him only by his sprightly conversation, knew. We find her thus at seventeen (1652), in the earliest bloom of her beauty, the wife of a crippled invalid, her protector rather than her husband, in a circle of society as gay and unscrupulous in conversation as in morals, requiring all her precocious talent and wise and watchful sense to enforce consideration and respect from that youthful company of the Fronde. She succeeded, however, and this was her apprenticeship to prudence and circumspection, which was to be the business and the pride of her whole life. Scarron died (1660), and the position of the beautiful widow of twenty-five, with no means, became more precarious, more dangerous, than ever. Let us in fact picture her to ourselves in this early beauty, which Mlle. de Scudéry has faithfully described to us:—

"*Lyriane* (this is Mme. Scarron, who is represented in *Clélie* as the wife of the Roman Scaurus),—Lyriane was tall, with a splendid figure, but her height was not alarming, simply becoming. Her complexion was very smooth and beautiful, her hair a bright chestnut, very pretty, the nose well formed, the mouth well shaped. Her manner dignified, sweet, bright, and modest; and, to render her beauty still more strikingly perfect, she had the loveliest eyes in the world. They were black, sparkling, soft, passionate, and full of fun; there was something I cannot express in their glance: a sweet melancholy appeared in them at times, with its ever present charm; while playfulness also danced in them in turn, with all the attraction which happiness inspires."

All contemporary testimony agrees in regard to that beauty, that graceful deportment, that wit, and that strain of playfulness. "All who know her," says the *Grand Dictionnaire des Précieuses*, "are quite convinced that she is one of the most sprightly persons of Athènes."* And towards the end of her life she describes herself as "gay by nature, and sad from her position." This shows us a side of her character which seems at the present day to have escaped us, and which the letters of Mme. de Maintenon only hint at. Her letters give us only a glimpse of her mind; the taste, the high-bred tone, the perfect judgment, and the piquant style are there, but the spirit with which she animated society, the wit so discreetly interspersed in her stories and conversation, and which sparkled so brightly and delicately in her face when she spoke enthusiastically, as Choisy says, all this is lost or unnoticed in her letters. We have only a kind of outline, or engraving, of the wit of Mme. de Maintenon, with none of the rich colour.

A critical moment arrived for Mme. Scarron after the death of her husband, but all her friends hastened to serve her, and succeeded in doing so. She received a pension from the queen-mother, and was able for some years to enjoy life as she felt inclined. She became one of the Hospitalières† of the Place Royale, and there she met the best society; she was constantly at the Hotel d'Albret or the Hotel de Richelieu. Old, and at the height of her glory, she spoke of these years of youth and poverty as the happiest of her life.

"All my youth was very pleasant," she said to her maidens of Saint-Cyr: "I had no ambition, nor any of those passions which might have disturbed my enjoyment of that vain shadow of

---

* Paris.—TRANSLATOR'S NOTE.

† A sisterhood for ladies of noble rank.—TRANSLATOR'S NOTE.

happiness (worldly happiness); for although I have experienced poverty, and passed through conditions very different to that in which you now see me, I was contented and happy. I knew neither weariness nor chagrin; I was free. I went to the Hotel d'Albret or to the Hotel de Richelieu, sure of a kind reception, and of finding my friends assembled there, or else of attracting them to my own salon, by warning them that I would remain at home."

Was Mme. Scarron able to remain free from all suspicion of evil during all these long years of widowhood and semi-worldliness? Discussion on this subject appears to me mere idle curiosity, and I leave questions of this nature to more daring minds; it is sufficient for me, and it ought to be enough for all whose aim it is to inquire into the character of an eminent personage, that Mme. de Maintenon preserved on the whole a line of conduct which was altogether circumspect and seemly. The most serious evidence we have in her disfavour is an expression of her friend Ninon, on the subject of M. de Villarceaux, their common friend; but in regard to this very insinuation, Ninon admits that she does not know how far things went, and that Mme. Scarron always seemed to her "too awkward for love." Now this sounds well, nay, is almost a guarantee. The fact is, if we put malice aside, that Mme. Scarron, during these her years of greatest peril, appears never to have been moved by sentiment at all, never to have been excited by the emotions of her heart, and to have been restrained by two curbs which are the strongest of all, namely, her love of consideration and esteem, which from her own account was her dominant passion, and her strict and practical religion, from which she never swerved. "I possess," she has said, "a great support in my religion, which prevents me doing evil things, shields me from all frailties, and makes me hate all that might draw scorn upon me."

I can find no reason to doubt her statement, other than the unforeseen circumstances of her life.

In these her younger days, the chief trait of her character, and the distinguishing feature of her social position, may be thus defined : she was one of those women, who as soon as they gain a little advantage, have the wit and the cleverness to make such good use of it, that they succeed in every way, simply by making themselves always useful and necessary, and at the same time pleasant and agreeable. No sooner had she the *entrée* of a house than she was initiated into all its private arrangements as no one else was, and, by some subtle vocation she possessed, she soon unconsciously, and without having any right to such a position, became the moving power of that household. In fact, intimacy established, her friends knew no half measures ; she became at once the soul, the charm, the fascination of that house.

Such was Mme. de Maintenon among friends like Mme. d'Heudicourt and Mme. de Montchevreuil, at the Hotels d'Albret and Richelieu ; considerate and attentive to every one, and so obligingly kind, that Saint-Simon has very justly observed upon this trait, and has described it to us in his own inimitable way ; for, with all his unjust exaggerations and inaccuracies, we must not ignore the masterly strokes of honest rectitude in what he says of Mme. de Maintenon ; but the explanation he gives of this diligence to please is more harsh than is quite fair, and I would rather judge from what Mme. de Maintenon tells us herself. She represents herself to us (in her correspondence) as industrious and active, up at six o'clock every morning, busy with all her different occupations, because she loved them, not from any interested motives ; and in matters concerning her women friends, laying herself out to oblige them, that she might be loved by them, and distinguished for her amiability, and also from an impulse of self-glorification.

"In my tender years," she has said, "I was what people call a good child,—everybody loved me; *even my aunt's servants were charmed with me.* When I was older, I was placed in various convents: you know how much I was loved there by my teachers and companions, and always for the same reason, because my chief thought from morning to night was of how I could serve them or oblige them. When I lived with that poor cripple, I found myself in the world of fashion, where I was sought after and esteemed. The women loved me because I was gentle in society, and because I was more occupied about others than about myself. Men waited on me because I had the beauty and the grace of youth. I have had all kinds of experiences, but have always kept my reputation stainless. The admiration I received was rather a general friendship or esteem than love. I did not desire to be loved by any one in particular; I wished to be loved by everybody, to be spoken of with admiring respect, to be popular, and especially to be approved of by good people: this was my ideal."

And again, *apropos* of that restraint which she at all times imposed on herself, and of that subordination of all her inclinations to which she forced her nature:—

"But that cost me little when I thought of those praises, of that fame, which would be the fruit of my discipline. That was my hobby. I was not concerned about riches; I was above all thought of self-interest; I desired honour."

This confession gives us the chief key to Mme. de Maintenon's conduct during her early life: active, obliging, insinuating but not vulgar, entering with extreme sensibility into the trials and troubles of her friends, and anxious to aid them, not from pure friendship, nor from true sympathy, nor from any principle of tender devotion, but because above everything else she yearned for their good opinion, she of necessity grasped every likely means to advance herself higher in their esteem: this, at least, is my opinion of her. Material and positive interest always was of secondary consideration in her eyes, in spite of her straitened circumstances, and was ever subordinate to that other moral interest founded on the esteem in which she was held. She longed to be specially distinguished and admired by those among whom she lived, whoever they were, and desired that it might be said of her: "As a woman, she is unique!" In this lay all her coquetry, —a coquetry of the mind, which with advancing years became to her an ambition, a career. Of an indefatigable temperament and unwearying patience, yet if one made a demand upon her in any direction touching self-respect and honour, she would accede to that which would have been barely possible to another. When at a later period she had become the most indispensable person at the court of Versailles, the companion of the king, the resource of princes, the person whom no one in all that royal household could ignore for a single moment, she showed herself capable of miraculous self-restraint and forbearance. Wholly occupied with the affairs of those she did not love, she endured her slavery with a smiling grace which never failed. "For twenty-six years," she has said, "I never displayed the slightest impatience at any time."

Latterly, through one of those illusions of self-esteem, —illusions which are very natural,—she imagined herself endowed with some special gift which fitted her for the new part she had to play,—a gift which was but the result, the perfection, and the crown of all the *rôles* it had been her fate to perform from her youth up: she regarded her life as a miracle. She had been so often called an Esther, that she believed herself one in reality, destined by Providence to sanctify the king, even although she herself should be a martyr. When the ladies of Saint-Cyr pressed her, during her last retreat there, to write her life, she declined, saying, that it would be a story full of marvellous inner experiences, and peculiar traits,—" Only saints would be able to find pleasure in reading it." And in expressing herself thus, she really believed that she spoke humbly. But it is not necessary to be a saint in order to find pleasure in those secrets of the heart which she herself has frankly unveiled.

Mme. de Montespan was still the declared mistress of the king when she met Mme. Scarron at the house of Mme. d'Heudicourt, their common friend, and, finding her so active, such a devoted friend, so discreet and domesticated, yet with an honourable amount of dignity, she could not help thinking what an inestimable advantage it would be if she could have her to educate secretly the two illegitimate children she had given to Louis XIV. According to the notions of the time, such a choice was a species of honour. Mme. Scarron, however, had discernment enough to perceive the dubiousness of the position, and very justly considered the proposal from its correct aspect. "If these children are the king's children," she replied, "I shall be very happy; I could not without scruple take charge of Mme. de Montespan's children; so the king must command me,—this is all I have to say." The king commanded, and Mme. Scarron became the governess of the mysterious children.

Her character is well portrayed in the singular life she lived during these years (1670-72). She took a large isolated house in the neighbourhood of Vaugirard, and, unknown to all her friends, took up her residence there, devoting herself to her precious charges, directing their early education, their diet, acting as housekeeper and nurse,—everything, in fact; and at the same time keeping up her customs of morning visits to her friends, as if nothing at all uncommon was going on at the very doors of these fashionable friends; for at first it was necessary that no one should suspect that there was anything unusual. Gradually, however, the secret began to be less carefully guarded, and the cloud unrolled. The king, who went to see his children, then got to know Mme. Scarron; but the impression she made on him at first was not favourable. "In the beginning I was very displeasing to the king; he looked on me as a clever person, to whom it was necessary to speak very learnedly,—a most difficult individual in every respect." There had been a time when Mme. de Montespan had had to make great efforts to break the ice, and to insinuate this chosen friend into the good graces of the king: we can imagine her subsequent bitterness and wrath.

Here we might easily exhaust all plausible explanations and apologies, but we should never succeed in proving that Mme. de Maintenon (for by this time she was so styled) did not at a certain period play a double game: installed by Mme. de Montespan, apparently deeply interested in her passion and in all the troubles connected with it, writing to her, even, in March 1678, "The king is returning to you covered with glory, and I am infinitely concerned in your joy;" while at the same time she had already conceived projects of personal ambition. Probably she did not all at once entertain the idea of what no imagination could have conjectured: she certainly could never have imagined, even in her own heart, that she would one day become not the secret but the acknowledged wife of the monarch; she only felt the possibility of being able to exercise great influence over him, and she kept this aim in view. This extraordinary romance was woven thread by thread, guided by the most patient and adroit skill. As soon as Mme. de Maintenon had gained a footing at court, she began to try to make it appear that she was not made for court life, and that she remained against her inclinations. This was one of her stratagems, one which probably half deceived even herself. In her ever-recurring schemes and threats of retirement, I can find no better comparison for her than M. de Chateaubriand, who, as we know, was always longing to exchange the world for a hermitage, to flee from it back to his American savages.

"I would return to America," said Mme. de Maintenon, "if I were not ceaselessly told that God requires me to remain where I am."

Her confessor was the Abbé Gobelin, who was clever enough to say to her very early, when indicating to her the place (a nameless place, and not even a vacant one, for the queen still lived) which had to be filled towards Louis XIV., "*God wishes you there!*" Mme. de Maintenon was persuaded, and remained, and nothing is more curious than to look at her between the two mistresses of the king (Mme. de Montespan and Mme. de Fontanges), reconciling one, counselling the other; conciliating, and, without seeming to do so, meddling with their affairs, and undermining them, and all the time (for this was her method, her weakness), craving pity for her situation, and continually expressing her wish to retire. Was there ever more skilful tact than this? Never did a woman's tact affect greater modesty or more refinement. "Nothing is more clever than irreproachable behaviour," Mme. de Maintenon has said, applying the expression to her own conduct. She may congratulate herself and glorify herself as she will, but I shall never call this virtue.

In the midst of her own peculiar and interesting affairs, she continued to exercise her characteristic influence. A true, warm-hearted woman would not for a single instant have accepted or endured such a *rôle*. Mme. de Maintenon spun out these ambiguous interests during many years.

"The king has three mistresses," said Mme. de Montespan to her furiously,—"myself in name, that girl (Fontanges) in fact, and you in the real affections of his heart." "His Majesty visits me occasionally, but not by my desire; he retires *disconsolate, but never hopeless,*" replied Mme. de Maintenon, in her triumphant humility. Or, on another occasion, she said: "I send him away *distressed always, but never despairing.*" This Penelope's web was woven and unwoven continually for about eleven years. Let us try to imagine the skill and invention, the wise discretion, which preserved for such a period the king's attachment, contenting him, yet not extinguishing his passion for her!

If, on a little consideration, we can see in Mme. de Maintenon, this woman of forty-five, the most consummate schemer, able so skilfully to carry on an intrigue in which passion and sentiment mingled under a cloak of virtue and religion, we must also recognise the intellectual talent she must have used, the conversational charm by which she amused, fascinated, and evaded a king less ardently in love than of old, and who is rather astonished to find himself attracted by a reluctance new to him. When the queen died unexpectedly in 1683, Mme. de Maintenon saw before her a vista of undreamt-of ambition, and she acted in this crisis as judiciously as she had heretofore acted, with prudent calculation disguised by supreme modesty. She was at last married secretly to the king, the date being, it is supposed, 1685. There were three or four persons, including her confessor, who in private called her "Your Majesty;" this satisfied her pride. As regarded all other people, it was sufficient for her, that she was a personage, distinct though not definite, occupying a place apart, respected, and enjoying her greatness, scarcely veiled by the cloud which covered it, conscious of the fulfilment of the marvellous destiny which, as Saint-Simon says, was conspicuous enough under its transparent mystery. Here, as in everything, there was a mixture of glory and modesty, of reality and sacrifice, which suited her well, and was her ideal ambition.

In her own words, which express so well her clear understanding, she defines her position on one occasion at Saint-Cyr, when, some one seeing her fatigued from unnecessary exercise, remarked in her presence that she was not careful enough of herself, did not comport herself as other great ladies: "That is because I am not *great*," she said; "I am only exalted."

Among the many portraits of Mme. de Maintenon, the one in my opinion which gives us the best idea of her in that last studied attitude of veiled greatness, is a portrait [No. 2258] which may be seen at Versailles, in one of the Queen's apartments. She is more than fifty, dressed in black, still beautiful, grave, and moderately stout, her high and noble forehead shaded by a veil. Her eyes are large and almond-shaped, very expressive, and wonderfully sweet. The nose is well formed and pleasing; the slightly dilated nostril indicates strength of mind. The still fresh mouth is small and gracious, and the chin, almost a double chin, well rounded. The sombre dress is just lightened by a drapery of white lace on the arms and shoulders. A high stomacher hides the neck. Such was Mme. de Maintenon,—almost a queen,—imposing, yet modest and self-restrained, —she who has said of herself: "My condition never shows me its brilliant aspect, but always its dark and painful side."

In that exalted position, what service has Mme. de Maintenon rendered to Louis XIV. or to France? To France, none—if we except the day that she requested Racine to write a sacred play for Saint-Cyr.* To Louis XIV. himself she rendered the service of weaning him from love intrigues which age would have made discreditable; she interested herself in everything she considered necessary for his best welfare: so far as human being could, she filled his time, amused him, and, as far as circumstances would allow, she provided hourly occupation for him; once admitted into the royal family circle, she displayed with even increased energy and exactitude that inexhaustible adaptability which, as a younger woman, had made her so useful to the Montchevreuils, the Heudicourts, and the Richelieus. She was indispensable in every difficulty, advising, consoling, always accessible and pleasant, in that royal home, amid all afflictions, amid all State affairs. This, rather than any political part, was the influence she wielded, although she may have intermeddled too much once or twice when family interests clashed, as in the preferment of the Duc du Maine. We know that Louis XIV. was possessed of sound judgment; but, as he advanced in years, that justice remained but inactive, uninventive, and was exercised only in affairs submitted to him, and according to the terms in which these matters were laid before him on the Council table; he took no trouble to search into affairs. Mme. de Maintenon, equally just, was also equally circumscribed; her interests were confined to social matters, or things of a purely private or family nature,—she neither saw nor prognosticated

* Esther.—Tr.

outside things. To sum up, neither of them was largeminded; they observed little outside the bounds of their own horizon, and the consequence was, that this horizon contracting with advancing years, this king, with all his sound judgment, committed many mistakes, which this woman of equal rectitude allowed him to commit, nay, even approved.

Mme. de Maintenon's judgment was quite proportionate to the king's; but his judgment inclined to the sombre side, whilst hers took the more cheerful view.

Did she love Louis XIV.? It would be cruel to raise any absolute doubt on this point. It seems, however, that of the two, he loved her the most, or, at all events, she was the more necessary to him. Dying, and when he had lost consciousness, we know that she withdrew before he had ceased to breathe; but, before leaving the expiring king, she desired, her confessor to see him, and to tell her if there was any hope of his regaining consciousness. "You may depart," said the confessor; "you are no longer necessary to him." She believed him, and obeyed, immediately leaving Versailles for Saint-Cyr. This act, for which she has been blamed, proves one thing only,—that she was a woman, who, in such a moment of supreme separation, trusted the advice of her confessor rather than the prompting of her own heart. Never for one moment in her whole life did Mme. de Maintenon lose control of her heart; there lies the secret of that certain degree of indifference she inspires. Her nature was altogether unsympathetic. We admit that, during her long life, in the midst of all the secret satisfactions to her self-love, she was constantly required to suffer, to restrain her wishes. The descriptions she has given us of the almost slavish tortures she was called upon to endure, in the midst of all her grandeur, are true pictures, and make us almost pity her. From the moment she awoke till the moment she retired to rest, she had no respite; she was at everybody's service, the princes to whom she sacrificed herself, the king who would not have sacrificed his smallest convenience even for the sake of her he loved and honoured more than all. By no means young, she suffered great discomfort from the cold draughts in these vast rooms, but she could not take it upon herself to order a screen to be placed behind her chair, because the king came there, and any irregularity in the *coup d'œil* would have displeased him: "Rather perish, than destroy the general symmetry." All the quarrels, complications, dissensions, of the royal family fell on her shoulders. "I have not been racked by four horses, but by four princes," she said one day, in an excess of fatigue; and she was obliged to employ all the skill on which she piqued herself to turn aside all such annoyances in her own pleasant, charming manner; she kept only the thorns for herself. Add to all this, the multitude of business matters which passed through her hands, especially affairs of religion, and conscientious scruples; for, as Saint-Simon says, she believed herself the *universal abbess;* she used to call herself the bishop's business woman. She was the target for demands of all kinds, although she evaded as much as she could, calling herself a cipher, a nonentity, an *Agnes** in politics; but she was not believed, and importunate petitions arrived from all parts, intercepting even her passage to and fro, in spite of the precautions she took to render approach to her difficult. "Truly, my head is sometimes almost turned," she said once, when she had nearly broken down; "and I believe

* Agnes, in Molière's comedy, *L'école des Femmes*, pretends to be wholly unsophisticated.—TRANSLATOR'S NOTE.

that if my body were opened after my death, my heart would be found hard and twisted like that of M. de Louvois." Let us not be too severe, then, in our judgment of this poor heart, which she lays bare to us. She is right, in one sense, to compare herself to a Louvois, to great statesmen, ambitious men: I do not think any one has ever carried the spirit of perseverance further than she did, or the art of circumspection, or the power of self-restraint.

Woman-like, she used strong language to describe that weariness of worry and annoyance which she was forced to endure, and obliged to conceal with a smile. "I am sometimes *gorged* with worries, as one might say." We recall her expression as she one day stood looking at some unhappy little fishes, very restless and uncomfortable in their clean basin of clear fresh water: "They are like me, they yearn after their obscurity."

But it was at Saint-Cyr that Mme. de Maintenon especially preferred to take refuge when she had a short interval of leisure, to hide herself, to give way to her feelings, to complain, and to be pitied, to reflect on her incomprehensible elevation, to pose as a victim bearing the weight of the kingdom's troubles. "Oh! say," she would exclaim, "is not the condition of Jeanne Brindelette d'Avon" (some little peasant pupil) "preferable to mine?"

Are not these the plaints of an ambitious woman, greedy of praise, complaining like the usurer of Horace, who, after extolling the charms of the country, quickly returns to town, and plans his money out at larger interest?

Listening to these royal wailings from Mme. de Maintenon's lips, and calling to mind her early prospects, we sometimes find ourselves quoting, with a smile, from Tartufe, "*The poor woman! the poor woman!*" And, after we have listened to her a little longer, we end by saying with her seriously, "*Yes, poor woman, indeed!*" Towards the end, it was apparent that she required such pity, for physical fatigue overbalanced all else, and the death of Louis XIV. was, to a certain degree, a relief to her.

There are two things for which, in the eyes of posterity, she must ever be commendable: first, the founding of Saint-Cyr; and secondly, her talent as an excellent writer. Saint-Cyr would require a separate study. Mme. de Maintenon stamped it with her own individuality, and she there shines as if set in a framework made expressly for her. It was there she was able to satisfy her craving to train and educate the young around her,—Minerva-like or Mentor-like tastes, which developed more and more as years advanced; she was also able there to unbend to tenderness. It was her own scheme, her cherished, almost maternal work. "Nothing is dearer to me than my children of Saint-Cyr; *I love them all, even the very dust they make.*" It is always so beautiful, so noble a thought to found a school destined to educate and train, in pure and regular principles, the children of the poor, that we hesitate to express even the most respectful criticism. Louis XV., however, who was not deficient in common sense, was severe in his judgment of Saint-Cyr. "Mme. de Maintenon," he said, "with the most excellent intentions, made a mistake. These girls are brought up in such a way, that it will be necessary to make them all ladies of the palace, or else they will be useless and unhappy." It would indeed be surprising, if, in an institution formed under the sole influence of Mme. de Maintenon, some vain-glorious pride had not slipped in. Let it, however, suffice now to remember, to the honour of Saint-Cyr, that it was the cradle of *Esther* and *Athalie;* its birth was the occasion of these immortal works.*

Yet it is as a writer that we accord to Mme. de Maintenon all enduring reputation. There is no complete and altogether accurate edition of her Letters, but what we have allows us to establish a judgment, and confirms what Saint-Simon has so aptly said of her "gentle, just, expressive language, naturally eloquent and concise." This brevity, or happy conciseness of style, is peculiar to Mme. de Maintenon, or is shared only by Mme. de la Fayette. Neither indulged in the tedious, careless, irregular style common to all women (who were not Mme. de Sévigné) in the seventeenth century. Mme. de Maintenon deserves much of the credit of the reformation in style which the eighteenth century inherited. "I shall correct the faults in style which you remark in my letters," wrote the Duc du Maine to her; "but I believe that long sentences will mean with me long imperfections." Mme. de Maintenon spoke faultlessly. Words dropped from her lips as from her pen, correct, apt, with never a syllable of discord; one word added might make a perfect sentence dry and stiff. Mme. du Deffand, who in literature is of the same school, has very ably expressed the effect of Mme. de Maintenon's Letters; they could not be better defined:—

"Her Letters are thoughtful," she says; "there is much intellect expressed in simple language; but they are not animated, and they are far from being as cheerful and pleasing as those of Mme. de Sévigné: the latter are all passionate feeling and energy; she takes her part in everything, is interested in, affected by everything. Mme. de Maintenon is the extreme opposite: she tells of the greatest events, in which she played her part, with the most perfect calmness; one can see that she

---

* By Racine.—TR.

loves neither the king, nor her friends, nor relations, nor even her position; devoid of sentiment and imagination, she has formed no illusions, she knows the intrinsic value of everything; she is tired of life, and says, '*Only death will put an end to vexation and unhappiness.*' . . . The result of my reading is, that I have a high estimation of her virtue, and little of her heart, and no liking for her person; but I repeat, I still persist in believing that she is not false."

She does not indeed appear to be false; in her Letters she is only a little too discreet and cautious. In order to form a correct idea of Mme. de Maintenon, it is advisable, in reading her Letters, to supply them with a certain sprightliness of wisdom, a peculiar grace, which characterized her to the last, in the midst of her austerity, and which was part of her desire to please people when beside them, but which was not strong enough to reflect in her written words.

I have, however, only approached the subject of Mme. de Maintenon; she is a study one must not proceed too hurriedly with: I shall hope to return to it some day, when I discuss her along with Mme. des Ursins.

MADAME DE SÉVIGNÉ.

1829.

CRITICS, and particularly foreign critics, who in these later years have been the most severe judges of our two literary centuries, agree in acknowledging that the features which most distinguished them, the influences which we find reflected in a thousand ways, lending brilliancy and *éclat* to these epochs, was, first, the wit of social intercourse, the knowledge of the world and of men, the shrewd intelligence displayed in courtesy and in ridicule, the ingenious delicacy of sentiment, the piquant grace and the refined courtliness of the language. And, indeed, with certain reservations, and not including such names as Bossuet and Montesquieu, these are the most marked characteristics of French literature as compared to all other European literature. This honour, which has almost been made into a reproach against our nation, is fertile enough, and fair enough, for those who are able to understand and interpret it.

At the beginning of the seventeenth century, our civilisation (and consequently, our literature and our language) was immature and uncertain. Europe, just emerging from religious difficulties, and still influenced by the effects of the Thirty Years' War, had laboriously created a new order of politics. France had exhausted herself with civil discord. In court circles there were salons and *ruelles*,* and the wits who frequented them were already the fashion; but as yet nothing great or original had been produced by them, and people feasted to satiety on Spanish romances or Italian sonnets and pastorals. It was not till after Richelieu's time, after the Fronde, under the queen-mother,† and Mazarin, that suddenly, from the midst of the fêtes of Saint-Mandé and Vaux, from the salons of the Hotel de Rambouillet, or from the antechambers of the young king,‡ arose as if by miracle, three great intellects, three geniuses, diversely gifted, but all endowed with pure original talent, perfect sympathy of taste, and a happy gift of language, embellished by natural grace and delicate refinement, destined to usher in an epoch of such glory and brilliancy as has never been surpassed. Molière, La Fontaine, and Mme. de Sévigné belong to a literary generation which preceded that of which Racine and Boileau were the chief lights; and they are distinguished from these latter by several marked features, which belong as distinctly to the nature of their genius as to the date of their appearance. We feel that in the place they hold, as in their peculiar turn of wit, they have much more in common with the France which preceded the reign of Louis XIV., with the old language, and the old French humour; their education,

---

* *Ruelle*, a word in daily use in the seventeenth century, probably requires some explanation in the present day. The bed, a magnificently adorned structure, occupied the middle of one end of the room; near the foot, and dividing the apartment, stood a gilt balustrade, such as may still be seen in the room of Louis XIV. at Versailles. Each side of the bed within that reserved space was called the *ruelle*.—TR.

† Anne of Austria.—TR.   ‡ Louis XIV.—TR.

and their literary knowledge altogether, belongs more to that epoch, and if they are less appreciated by foreigners than certain subsequent writers, this is due in reality to the particular and indefinable charm which for us exists in the purity of their style and diction. Therefore, at the present time, we are reasonably anxious to revise and refute many of the judgments and opinions which, during the last twenty years, have been set for the professors of the Athenæum; and we declare relentless war against many who have been greatly overrated, and uphold those immortal writers who first gave to French literature its originality, and encouraged those characteristic features which, up to the present day, assure for it a distinct place among all other literatures. Molière drew from the moving game of life the vices and eccentricities of mankind; he depicts everything which could possibly be worthily expressed in poetry. La Fontaine and Mme. de Sévigné, in a narrower sphere, had each in their way an exquisitely true preception of all which concerned the spirit of their time. La Fontaine represented nature, Mme. de Sévigné was more the interpreter of society; and this delicate feeling they have both so clearly expressed in their writings, that quite naturally we compare them with, and scarcely rank them below, their illustrious contemporary. At present we desire to speak only of Mme. de Sévigné, and it seems as if nothing new could be said of her,—details regarding her are, in fact, almost exhausted; but we think that hitherto, in studying her, she has been too much isolated, just as La Fontaine was for a long time, and to him she bears a strong resemblance. At this distance of time, when the society of which she represents the most brilliant aspect is distinctly and harmoniously revealed to our eyes, it is easier, as at the same time it becomes more necessary, to assign to Mme. de Sévigné her rank, her importance, and especially her relation to other writers ; this, and the difference of the times, has not been sufficiently borne in mind by the many distinguished writers of our own day, who are disposed to judge with equal carelessness and severity one of the most charming geniuses who ever existed. We shall be glad if this sketch help to dissipate some of those unjust prejudices.

The excesses of the *Regency* have been much censured ; but before the regency of Philippe d'Orleans there was another regency, not less dissolute, and still more atrocious, by reason of the cruelties with which it is associated, —a kind of hideous transition state between the flood of abuses perpetrated by Henri III. and those of Louis XV. The low morality of the Ligue, which had smouldered under Henri IV. and Richelieu, revived again, being no longer restrained. Licentiousness became as excessive as it had been in the days of the *mignons*, or as it was later in the time of the *roués;* but what makes this epoch most resemble the sixteenth century, and distinguishes it from the eighteenth, is chiefly the assassinations, poisonings, and other Italian vices due to the influences of the Médicis, and the insane rage for duelling — a heritage of the civil wars. Such, to the impartial reader, appears the regency of Anne of Austria, and such was the dark and bloody basis ·on which, one fine morning, loomed the Fronde, which it is considered proper to call *une plaisanterie à main armée.** The conduct of the women of the time, those most distinguished by their birth, their beauty, and their wit, seems incredible, and we are forced to believe that historians have slandered them. But as excess always produces its contrary, the small number of them who escaped corruption embraced sentimental metaphysics,

* The trick of an armed hand.

and became *Précieuses*.* The Hotel de Rambouillet was the abode of good morals within the pale of the highest society; whilst its good taste must now be admitted, since it has produced Mme. de Sévigné.

Mlle. Marie de Rabutin-Chantal was the daughter of the Baron de Chantal, whose uncontrolled passion for duelling led him, one Easter Day, to quit the Holy Table to go and act as second to the famous Comte de Bouteville. Brought up by her uncle, the good Abbé de Coulanges, she early received very solid instruction, and learnt, under Chapelain and Ménage, the Latin, Italian, and Spanish languages. At eighteen she married the Marquis de Sévigné, little worthy of her; who, after grossly neglecting her, was killed in a duel in 1651. Widowed at five-and-twenty, the mother of a son and daughter, Mme. de Sévigné had no idea of marrying again; she loved her children, especially her daughter, almost foolishly, and other persons remained unknown to her. She was fair and gay, a smiling picture of virtuous womanhood; the brilliancy of her wit gave lustre to her expressive eyes, shone from her ever-changing pupils, and; as she herself said, was luminous even behind the curtain of her transparent eyelids. She became a *Précieuse*; she went into society, was beloved, courted,† an object of unheeded passion, brave enough to preserve as friends

---

* A term of eulogy bestowed upon the circle of intellect and beauty which surrounded the Marquise de Rambouillet, who herself received from her admirers the title of the Incomparable Arthénice. To be styled a *Précieuse* was a high mark of distinction, although afterwards ridiculed by Molière's "Précieuses ridicules."

† Mme. de la Fayette wrote to her: "Your presence adds to diversion, and diversion enhances your beauty. In short, joy is the natural state of your soul, and sorrow is more unnatural in you than in any other."

those she would not listen to as lovers. Her cousin
Bussy, her tutor Ménage, the Prince of Conti, brother
of the Grand Condé, Fouquet, the powerful Surintendant,
all sighed in vain for her, although she remained
courageously faithful to the latter in his disgrace ; and
when she tells M. de Pomponne of his prosecution, we
must observe how tenderly she speaks of "our dear
unfortunate." Still young and beautiful and unassum-
ing, she appeared in society only as the devoted mother,
caring for no greater happiness than that of exhibiting
her daughter and seeing her admired.* Mlle. de
Sévigné took part from 1663 in the brilliant ballets
of Versailles ; and Benserade, court poet, who then
held at court the place which Racine and Boileau took
after 1672, wrote more than one madrigal in honour
of that shepherdess and nymph, who was called by
her idolizing mother the loveliest maiden in France.
In 1669, M. de Grignan obtained her hand in marriage,
and sixteen months afterwards she accompanied him
to Provence, where he acted as lieutenant-general
during the absence of M. de Vendome. From henceforth separated from her daughter, whom she saw
only at long irregular intervals, Mme. de Sévigné
sought to make her loneliness less irksome by a constant
correspondence, which lasted till her death (in 1696),
and which extends over twenty-five years, excepting
the gaps which are filled in by the transient reunions

* There is a beautiful portrait of Mme. de Sévigné in her
youth by the Abbé Arnauld, who says in his Mémoires that he
was introduced to the illustrious Mme. de Sévigné. . . . "I can
fancy that I see her still," he says, "as she appeared to me the
first time I had the honour of beholding her. She arrived in an
open chariot, on either side of her sat her son and daughter, all
three such as poets paint,—Latona with the young Apollo and the
child Diana,—so striking was the beauty of mother and children."

of the mother and daughter. Before this separation we have only a very few letters of Mme. de Sévigné's addressed to her cousin Bussy, and some to M. de Pomponne about the prosecution of Fouquet. It is, therefore, only from this date that we possess any intimate knowledge of her private life, her habits, her favourite books, and even minute details of the society she lived in, and of which she was the soul.

And from the very first pages of this correspondence we find ourselves in quite a different world from that of the Fronde and the Regency; we recognise that what is called French society is at last constituted. Doubtless (and beside the numerous mémoires of the time, the anecdotes related by Mme. de Sévigné herself are our authority), horrible licentiousness, gross orgies, were indulged in by the young noblesse, on whom Louis XIV. imposed, as the price of his favour, the exercise of politeness, elegance, and dignity; no doubt, under this brilliant superficiality, this gilding of the Carrousel, there was quite enough inherited vice ready to manifest itself anew in another regency, especially when the bigotry of the last years of this reign should have caused it to ferment. But at least outward propriety was observed; public opinion began to disparage things ignoble or dissolute. Moreover, as disorder and vicious passion became less scandalous, decency and refined wit gained in simplicity. The title *Précieuse* went out of fashion, or was remembered with a smile. People no longer declaimed in private, and commented on the sonnet of Job, or of Uranie on the map of *Tendre* * or on the Roman character; but they conversed, they talked over the news of the court, conversed of the siege of Paris, or of the wars of Guienne: the Cardinal de Retz

* In the love stories of the seventeenth century, *Tendre* was the name given to an allegorical Kingdom of Love.—Tr.

described his travels; M. de la Rochefoucauld moralized; Mme. de la Fayette made sentimental reflections; and Mme. de Sévigné interrupted them all to quote some clever saying of her daughter, some roguish trick of her son, some absent-mindedness of the good D'Hacqueville or of M. de Brancas.

In 1829, with our regular habits and occupations, we have some difficulty in faithfully picturing to ourselves this life of leisure and conversation. The world goes on so fast in our time, and so many things are in turn brought upon the scene, that it takes us all our time to behold and apprehend them. Our days are passed in study, our evenings in serious discussions, friendly intercourse, and conversation. The nobility of our day, which has preserved most of the leisurely habits of the two last centuries, seems to have been able to do this only at the cost of remaining strangers to the thoughts and customs of the present time.* At the date of which we write, far from there being any difficulty in following the literary, political, or religious spirit of the day, it was the correct mode and purpose of life; a glance of the eye was sometimes enough, an aside whilst indulging in familiar friendly talk. Conversation had not then become, as in the eighteenth century, in the open salons, under the presidency of Fontenelle, an occupation, a business full of pretension; no one specially aimed at making clever hits, or at ostentatiously displaying his eloquent knowledge of geometry, philosophy, or sentiment; but people conversed of

* Since these pages were written, I have frequently had occasion to remark to myself, and with great pleasure, that this decay of conversational power in France has been rather exaggerated; no doubt, it is absent as a general rule in society, but there are still remnants of it, an after-glow, which is all the more enjoyable that it seems the revival of a lost art.

themselves, of others, of little or of nothing at all. It was, as Mme. de Sévigné said, endless conversation. "After dinner," she writes in one letter to her daughter, "we went and chatted in the most pleasant wood in the world; we remained there till six o'clock, engaged in every variety of converse, kindly, pleasing, amiable, and affectionate, both for you and for me, so that I was much impressed." In the midst of this impulsive society, so simple and easy, and so gracefully animated, a visit, a letter received, was an event from which much pleasure might be extracted, and in which every one eagerly took part. The most trifling things were valued according to the mode or the form in which they were presented; this was the art which unconsciously and carelessly pervaded life. Let us recall to our minds the visit Mme. de Chaulnes paid to the *Rochers*.

It has often been said that Mme. de Sévigné was curiously careful of her letters, and that, in writing them, she thought, if not of posterity, at least of the people of her time whose approbation she sought. This is untrue; the time of Voiture and of Balzac was already far distant. She usually wrote with great fluency, allowing her pen to run on, on all kinds of subjects; and, when pressed for time, scarcely ever re-reading what she wrote. "Truly," she has said, "between friends we must let our pens wander at will; mine always has a loose rein." But there are days when she has more leisure, and when she feels more in the mood; then quite naturally she arranges and composes her letters with almost as much care as La Fontaine bestows on one of his fables.

Such was the letter to M. de Coulanges, on the marriage of Mademoiselle; such the one about the unfortunate Picard, who was dismissed because he refused to join in the haymaking. Letters such as these, brilliant as works of art, and in which there are not too many little secrets nor slanders, made a sensation in society; every one wished to read them. "I cannot help telling you what happened this morning," writes Mme. de Coulanges to her friend: "I was told that one of Mme. de Thianges' pages had called; I gave orders for his admission. This is what he had to say to me: 'Madame, my mistress begs you to send her two letters of Mme. de Sévigné's, the letter *du cheval* and the one of the *Prairie.*' I told the page that I would take them to Mme. de Thianges, and so got rid of him. Your letters are as famous as they deserve to be, as you see. They certainly are delicious, and you are like your letters." Correspondence, therefore, like conversation, was of great importance; but neither the one nor the other was composed, they were spontaneous utterances of heart and mind. Mme. de Sévigné constantly praises her daughter's letters. "Your ideas are beautiful, your sentences incomparable," she says; and she tells how she reads here and there from them, chosen passages, to those she considers worthy to hear them,—"Sometimes I also read a little bit from them to Mme. de Villars, but she is so much touched by the tender parts that tears come into her eyes."

If the unaffected simplicity of Mme. de Sévigné's letters has been disputed, so also has the sincerity of her love for her daughter been doubted; and, in judging of this affection, allowance has not been made for the time she lived in, and we are apt to forget that, in that luxurious age, passions were like whims, and over-fondness often became a passion. She idolized her daughter, and at once made this understood in society. Arnauld d'Andilly called her, on this account, a *pretty pagan*. Separation but increased her tenderness; it almost entirely filled her thoughts, and the inquiries and

compliments of all her friends continually reverted to
this absorbing subject: this cherished and almost
unique affection of her heart at length became a very
part of her demeanour, as necessary in her deportment
as the fan she carried. After all, Mme. de Sévigné
was perfectly sincere and open, and despised pretence,
a *real woman*, — an expression she would doubtless
have invented for her daughter, had not M. de la
Rochefoucauld already discovered it for Mme. de la
Fayette; she, however, pleased herself by adopting it
for her she loved. When we have thoroughly analyzed
and examined in every light this boundless mother-
love, we simply return to M. de Pomponne's opinion
and explanation: "Mme. de Sévigné appears to
have loved Mme. de Grignan passionately. Would
you like to know the real fact of the matter? Well,
she loves her passionately." It would, in truth, be very
ungrateful to carp at Mme. de Sévigné on account of
this innocent and most legitimate passion, to which we
are indebted for our power of accompanying, step by
step, this most brilliantly clever woman during twenty-
six years of the most agreeable epoch of French social
history.*

La Fontaine, nature's painter, does not altogether
neglect and ignore society; he frequently depicts it
with subtle malice. Mme. de Sévigné, on her part, loved

---

* M. Walckenaer aptly remarks in his Mémoires of Mme. de
Sévigné: "She in whom the maternal sentiment was so strongly
developed, never had the opportunity of possessing the filial
sentiment, having been so early orphaned. All the love of her
heart was held in reserve, to be showered on her daughter.
Widowed in the spring-time of her youth and beauty, she seems
never to have cared for any of those who courted her. What a
treasury of love! And her daughter inherited it all, with its
accumulated interest."

nature; she delighted in the country, and made long sojourns at Livry with the Abbé de Coulanges, or on her own estate, the Rochers, in Brittany; and it is very interesting to observe her impressions of nature. We at once perceive that, like our good fabulist, she had early read *L'Astrée*, and we find traces of girlish dreams under the mythological shades of Vaux and St. Mandé. She loves to wander under the bright rays of Endymion's mistress, or spend hours alone with the *hamadryads* (wood nymphs). Her trees are covered with inscriptions and curious mottoes, as in the landscapes of *Pastor fido* and the *Aminte*. "*Bella cosa far niente*, says one of my trees, and the other replies, *Amor odit inertes* (Love hates idlers). We know not which to listen to." And elsewhere she remarks: "They are not disfigured by our sentences; I often visit them; they are even augmenting, and two neighbouring trees will often say quite contrary things: *La lontananza ogni gran piaga salda*, and *Piaga d'amor non si sana mai*. There are five or six thus contradictory." These reminiscences of pastoral romances, a little insipid though they are, flow quite naturally from her pen, and pleasantly relieve the many fresh and original descriptions she so charmingly writes. "I have come here" (to Livry) "to see the end of the fine weather, and bid adieu to the leaves. They are still on the trees, and have but changed colour; instead of being green, they are golden, of so many varied tints that they form a brocade, so gorgeous and magnificent that we are tempted to prefer it to the green, if only by way of change." And again, when she is at the Rochers, she writes: "I should be so happy in these woods, if the foliage would but sing; oh, how lovely it would be to listen to the warbling leaves!" And again, how glowing is her description of the *rapturous month of May, when the nightingale, the cuckoo, and the warbler usher in the spring-time in our woods and forests!* how intensely she can make us feel,—nay, how she permeates our being with the very touch of those *beautiful crystal days of autumn, which are no longer warm, and yet not cold!* When her son, to meet his foolish extravagances, causes the old woods of Buron to be cut down, she rebels, and grieves with all the banished dryads and ousted fauns; Ronsard could not more worthily have deplored the disappearance of the forest of Gastine, nor M. de Chateaubriand the hewing down of his paternal woods.

Because we often find her in a gay and sportive mood, we must not be unjust, and judge that Mme. de Sévigné is frivolous or unfeeling. She was serious, even sad, especially during her sojourns in the country; all her life she was subject to long fits of reverie. Only, we must understand, she did not dream under the shade of those thick dark avenues after the manner of Delphine, or in the mood of Oswald's sweetheart: that peculiar form of reverie had not yet been invented; Mme. de Staël had not yet written her admirable book, *The Influence of Passion upon Happiness.* At this time reverie was a simpler matter, a personal and quite unconscious condition of mind; it meant thoughtful musing of her daughter far away from her in Provence, of her son in Candia or with the king's army, of her distant or dead friends; it suggested thoughts expressed as follows: "As regards my life, you know what it is: passed with five or six friends, whose society is pleasing to me, in the exercise of a thousand necessary duties, which require time. But what vexes me is, that in doing nothing, our days pass, and our poor existence is composed of such days, and we grow old and die. I find this very cruel." The exact and regular religious observances which governed her life did much at that time to temper the free play of her imagination, which afterwards on religious subjects she did not curb, although she carefully guarded herself against some thoughts which we must pass over. She earnestly sought after Christian doctrines and Christian principles, and more than once accused her daughter of being tainted with Cartesianism.* For herself, as regards the unforeseen, she bowed her head, and took refuge in a kind of providential fatalism, with which her connection with Port-Royal, and her studies of Nicole and St. Augustin had inspired her.

This resigned religious element in Mme. de Sévigné's character increased with years without changing in the slightest degree the serenity of her disposition; it often communicated to her language a graver, more judicious tenderness. This is especially observable in a letter to M. de Coulanges on the death of Louvois, in which her sublime eloquence equals Bossuet, as in other days and in other circumstances she had almost surpassed the humour of Molière.

M. de Saint-Surin, in his esteemed work on Mme. de Sévigné, lost no opportunity of comparing her to Mme. de Staël, and invariably gave her the advantage over that famous woman. We agree that it is both

* There have been many disputes as to the merits of Mme. de Grignan, and probably her mother has harmed her a little in our eyes by praising her too much; it forces one into a difficult position with uninterested persons to be made an object of too much love. The son, who was rather rakish, seems to us much more amiable. According to my ideas, we can easily understand how the good sense and gaiety of Mme. de Sévigné's nature were divided, and, as it were, distributed between her children: one, the son, inherited her gracious ways, but not much sense or solidity; the other, the daughter, had the sense, but her apparent brusqueness was not softened by any charming sprightliness of temper.

interesting and profitable to make this comparison, but it need not be to the detriment of either. Mme. de Staël represents an entirely new society, Mme. de Sévigné a banished society ; from this fact arises the stupendous differences, which one is at first tempted to explain solely by the dissimilarity of mind and nature. However, and without any desire to deny this profound and original dissimilarity between two hearts, one of which understood only maternal love, while the other had experienced every passion the most generous and the bravest, we find in them, on close examination, many common weaknesses, many common virtues, which owe only their different development to the difference of time. What genuine ability, full of airy grace, what glowing pages of pure wit, in Mme. de Staël, when sentiment does not play a part, and when she allows philosophy and politics to slumber! And Mme. de Sévigné—does she never philosophize, never declaim ? If not, of what use her study of such books as the *Morale* of Nicole, the *Socrate chrétien*, and St. Augustin ? For this woman, who has been looked upon as shallow and frivolous, read everything, and read with perfect comprehension and sympathy : "It gives," she said, "a *pale colour to the mind* to take no pleasure in solid reading." She read Rabelais, Montaigne and Pascal, Cleopatra and Quentilien, Saint Jean Chrysostom, and Tacitus and Virgil,—not travestied versions, she enjoyed them *in all the majesty of the Latin* and Italian. In rainy weather she would get through a folio in less than a fortnight. During Lent, she loved to listen to Bourdaloue.*
Her attitude towards Fouquet, in his disgrace, makes us realize the devotion she was capable of displaying in the days of revolution. If she shows a little vanity or conceit, when the king one evening dances a minuet

* An eloquent preacher of the day.—Translator's Note.

with her, or when he pays her a gracious compliment at Saint-Cyr, after the performance of (Racine's) *Esther*, who among her sex would, in her place, have been more philosophical? Did not Mme. de Staël herself take a great deal of trouble to obtain a word, a glance, from the conqueror of Egypt and Italy (Napoleon). Surely a woman who, from her earliest youth, had associated with such men as Ménage, Godeau, and Benserade, her own good sense alone protecting her from their insipid compliments and witticisms; able playfully to evade the refined, seductive attentions of such as Saint-Evremond and Bussy; a woman who was the friend and admirer of Mlle. de Scudéry and of Mme. de Maintenon, and who yet preserved her own individuality, as far removed from the romantic sentiment of the one as from the too reserved severity of the other; who, connected by many ties with Port-Royal, fed, as it were, on the works of these *Messieurs*, and who modestly hid her knowledge of Montaigne, never even quoting Rabelais, and desiring no other inscription for what she called *son couvent*, than *Sainte liberté*, or *Fais ce que voudra*, as at the Abbey of Thélème,—such a woman is free to indulge in sportive, playful moods, to allow her thoughts to *glide*, to amuse herself by seeing things from their most familiar aspect; she proves her profound energy and the rare originality of her wit.

There is only one occasion on which we cannot help regretting that Mme. de Sévigné allowed herself to indulge in frivolous, mocking expressions; an occasion on which we absolutely refuse to enter into her badinage, which, indeed, even after taking into consideration every extenuating circumstance, we can scarcely pardon. It is when she so gaily describes to her daughter the revolt of the Breton peasants, and the horrible severities with which it was repressed. So long as she confines herself to mocking the States, the country squires, laughing at their amazing feasts, and enthusiastic haste to get over the voting between mid-day and one o'clock, and all the other follies of her Breton neighbours after dinner, it is all very well, a proper and legitimate kind of fun, which in some places recalls the flavour of Molière. But as soon as the trenches are opened in the province, and a *colique pierreuse* is reported from Rennes—that is to say, when the governor, M. de Chaulnes, wishing to disperse the people by his presence, has been driven back to his house by stones; from the moment M. de Forbin arrives with six thousand soldiers against the rioters, and when the poor devils, seeing the royal troops in the distance, disband and try to escape through the fields, or throw themselves on their knees, crying *Mea culpa*, for they know no French, only their own patois; when, to punish Rennes, its Parlement was removed to Vannes; when five-and-twenty or thirty men, taken haphazard, were hanged; when they drove into banishment all the inhabitants of one great street, sick women, old men, and little children, forbidding any one to shelter them under pain of death, torturing by the rack and the wheel, and then setting the victims free by hanging them,—in the midst of such horrors, perpetrated against poor, innocent, homeless people, it pains us to find Mme. de Sévigné making playful remarks, almost as on some ordinary subject. We should expect her to be full of generous, angry indignation; but above all we should like to erase from her letters lines like these: "The rebels of Rennes escaped long ago, so the innocent suffer for the guilty; but it is all right, provided the four thousand soldiers who are at Rennes, under MM. de Forbin and de Vins, do not hinder me from wandering about in my woods, which I find marvellously grand

and solemnly beautiful." And elsewhere : "They have arrested sixty townsmen, and to-morrow they begin to hang. This province is a good example to others, particularly to teach respect for governors, not to insult them, nor to throw stones in their gardens." And again, and lastly : "You speak very complacently of our distress ; we are no longer *si roués*,* the rack once a week is sufficient for justice, mere hanging seems a refreshing process now." The Duc de Chaulnes, who urged all this vengeance because some one had thrown stones in his garden, and said some insulting things to him, of which the mildest was *fat pig*, was not lowered an atom in the good graces of Mme. de Sévigné ; he remained to her always, and to Mme. de Grignan, who was as devoted to him, "our good Duke ;" more than this, when he was appointed ambassador at Rome, and left the province, all Brittany was overwhelmed with sorrow. Certainly, we have here matter for much reflection on the customs and civilisation of the great century ; our readers can easily fill in the gap. We can only regret that on this occasion Mme. de Sévigné was not superior to her time ; she might worthily have been so, for her kindness of heart equalled her beauty and grace. It happened occasionally that she desired to recommend a convict to the merciful consideration of M. de Vivonne or M. de Grignan. The most interesting of these *protégés* was certainly a gentleman of Provence, whose name has not been preserved. "This unfortunate youth," she wrote, " was attached to the service of M. Fouquet, and was convicted of having rendered him the service of transmitting a letter from him to Mme. Fouquet ; for this he has been condemned to the galleys for five years. This is a rather unusual case. You understand, he is one of the most honest fellows one could meet with,

* So much broken on the wheel as we were.

and as fit for the galleys as to try and take the moon by the horns."

Mme. de Sévigné's style has been so often and so ably judged, analyzed, admired, that it is difficult now to find any words of praise which would be at the same time new and suitable to apply to her; and, on the other side, we do not feel at all disposed to revive the commonplace by cavil and criticism. A single general observation will suffice; it is, that we may ascribe the grand and beautiful styles of Louis the XIV.'s time to two different methods, two distinct and opposing mannerisms. Malherbe and Balzac endowed our literature with its learned, masterly polish, in the creation of which the faculty of expression arose, though gradually, slowly, after many hesitating efforts. This careful style Boileau took every opportunity of encouraging: "Revise your work twenty times," he says; "polish and repolish it unweariedly." He boasts of having with difficulty taught Racine to make fluent verses. Racine may be considered the most perfect model of this highly polished style. Fléchier was less happy in his prose than Racine as a poet. But, distinct from this manner of composition, in which there is always a certain academical uniformity, there exists another very different style, fickle, unconstrained, and versatile, following no traditional method, conformable to all diversities of talent and to every variety of genius. Montaigne and Regnier have furnished us with excellent examples of this style, and Queen Marguerite * has given us one charming specimen in her familiar Mémoires, the work of a few after-dinner hours. This is the full, wide, flowing style, which better suits the present taste,—impulsive, off-hand, so to speak, like Montaigne himself; the style also of La Fontaine, Molière, of Fénelon and Bossuet, of the Duc de Saint-

* Of Savoy.

Simon and of Mme. de Sévigné. A style in which the latter excels, she allows her pen to *run along with a very loose rein*, and as she goes on, she scatters her wealth of imagery, of comparison, and glowing colour, while wit and sentiment slip from her unawares. Thus, without effort, and with no suspicion of it herself, she takes first rank among the great writers in our language.

"The sole artifice of which I dare suspect Mme. de Sévigné," says Mme. Necker, "is that of frequently using general and consequently rather vague expressions, which, from her manner of arranging them, may be compared to a flowing robe, a shapeless garment, the fashion of which an artistic hand may model at will." The comparison is ingenious, but there is not necessarily any author's artifice in this style, common to her epoch. Before exactly adjusting itself, or adapting itself to such a vast variety of dissimilar ideas, the language has amplified its powers in all directions, and has thus become possessed of a rich facility of diction and a singular grace of phraseology. As soon as the epoch of analysis is past, and a language has been cut and carved, and elaborated into use, the indefinable charm is lost, and it is in the attempt to return to former conditions that real artifice consists.

And now, if in all we have said, we appear to some prejudiced minds to have carried our admiration for Mme. de Sévigné too far, will they allow us to ask them a question: Have you read Mme. de Sévigné? And by *reading* we do not mean running through some chance collection of her letters, not merely forming an opinion from two or three which enjoy a classical renown, —such as her letters on the intended marriage of Mademoiselle, on the death of Vatel, of M. de Turenne, of M. de Longueville,—but going thoroughly, page by page, through the ten volumes of letters (and we specially recommend the edition of M. Monmerqué and M. de Saint-Surin), following, to use her own expression, *every thread* of her ideas. Read her, in fact, as you would *Clarissa Harlowe*, when you have a fortnight's rainy leisure in the country; and after this test, not a very terrible one, you will share in our admiration, if you have the courage to confess it, always supposing that it has been still remembered.

MADAME DE STAËL.

1835.

I.

When revolution has changed society, no sooner has the lowest depth been reached, than we begin lovingly to turn our thoughts backward, and to distinguish among the varied pinnacles soaring on the horizon, certain giant forms which hold themselves apart as the divinities of certain places. This personification of the genius of times in illustrious individuals is not a pure illusion of perspective; distance certainly favours such points of view, separates, perfects, but does not create them. There are true and natural representatives of every moment of social life; although, from a little distance, the number decreases, and detail becomes less complex, till at last only one prominent summit remains. *Corinne*, from afar, stands out distinct and clear on Cape Misene.*

The French Revolution, which in every crisis had its great men, possessed also its brilliant and heroic women, whose names are associated with the experiences of each successive phase. As the old society died out, it had its innocent victims, its captives, who were crowned with a brilliant halo of glory in prisons or on scaffolds. The *bourgeoisie*, rising rapidly, produced very quickly

* An allusion to a scene in *Corinne.*—Tr.

their heroines, and also their victims. Later on, ere the storm had lulled, groups of famous women arose, who have glorified that reanimation of social life and the enjoyments of wealth. The Empire also had its distinguished women, exercising, however, at that time but little influence. At the Restoration we discover the name of some noble woman who worthily represents the manners and dispassionate opinions of the Empire. But the many successive celebrities who are closely connected with every phase of the Revolution, all at last find themselves grouped round one single celebrity, who includes them all within herself, reconciles them all together, participates in the brilliancy and devotion which appertains to them, takes her part in raising the standard of politeness and energy, sentiment and courage, inspiring intellect with noble aims, then encircling all these gifts by the genius which obtains for them immortal honour.

A child of the Reformation through her father, Mme. de Staël was linked by education, and by the traditions of her early youth, to the salons of the old world. The personages among whom she grew up, and who smiled on her precocious flight, were those who formed the most intellectual circle of these waning years of former times: reading about 1810, at the time she was most persecuted, the Correspondence of Mme. du Deffand and Horace Walpole, she found herself wonderfully moved at the remembrance of that great world, in which she had been acquainted with many famous people, and in which every family was known to her. If her early attitude, then, was remarkable for a kind of sentimental animation, which certain envious aristocrats censured, she was destined by the very impulsiveness of her eloquence to convince her hearers always and everywhere. But even in this quiet, peaceful circle she had already become an undoubted ornament, and she went forth to continue, on a less stereotyped but grander model, a series of salons as illustrious as were those salons of the old French *régime*. Mme. de Staël had inherited sufficient of the charm and of the manner of these former times; but she did not depend on that heritage, for, like most geniuses, she was distinguished in an unusually eminent degree for the universality of her intelligence, her capacity for affection, and a constant necessity for new sensations. Besides the traditional and already classic success of Mme. du Deffand and Mme. de Beauvau, which she had adopted as her style, blended with her own originality, she was inspired by the fresh energy, the plebeian genius, and the courage of the republican spirit. The heroism of Mme. Roland and Charlotte Corday found its echo in her heart; her exquisite sympathy with noble aspirations never failed. True sister of André Chénier by instinct and devotion, she had her eloquent cry of sorrow for the queen, as he uttered his for the king (Louis XVI.), and she would have gone to the bar of justice to defend her had there been a remote chance of saving her. She suffered soon; and in her book on *The Influence of the Passions*, she expresses all the sadness of virtuous Stoicism in these times of oppression when one could do nothing but die.

Under the Directorate, her writings and her conversation, without excluding the preceding qualifications, are more severe in tone; she supports the cause of philosophy, of perfectibility, of a moderate and liberal republic, just as the widow of Condorcet might have done. It was a little later than in the preface to *Literature considered in connection with Social Institutions*, that she expressed this bold idea: "Some of Plutarch's lives, a letter of Brutus to Cicero, some of the words of Cato of Attica in the language of Addison, some reflec-

tions with which hatred of tyranny inspired Tacitus,
revives the spirit which contemporaneous events would
blast." This did not hinder her from, at the same time,
showing the pleasure she took in the renewal of old
friendships as soon as they reappeared from exile. And
at this time she welcomed, and with all her heart appreciated, the fame of the most highly esteemed woman of
her time,* the purest, and the most accomplished; she
encircled herself with these friends as with a garland,
while *Les Lettres de Brutus* are still half read, and M. de
Montmorency smiles pityingly on her. Thus, step by
step, or at once, the intellectual impulse of the salons of
the eighteenth century, the vigour of new hopes and
large enterprises, the sadness of Stoic patriotism with
the renewing of gracious friendships, and the access to
modern elegance, influenced in various ways that soul
as changeable as it was truly complete. And later,
on her return to France, after the Empire, in the too
few years she lived, we find her grasping with equal
promptitude the meaning of necessary transactions,
while her frequent friendships in these times, with
persons like Mme. de Duras, furnish the last touch
required to give to her life every characteristic shade
of the social phases through which she passed, from the
half philosophical and innovating salon of her mother,
to the liberal royalty of the Restoration. Regarding it
from this point of view, Mme. de Staël's existence is
altogether like a great empire, which she is ceaselessly
occupied, no less than that other conqueror, her contemporary and oppressor, in completing and augmenting. But it is not in a material sense that she acts, it
is not province after province, and one kingdom after
another, that her indefatigable activity covetously requires; it is in the ordering of her mind that she

* Mme. Récamier.

ceaselessly expands; it is the multiplicity of noble ideas, of profound sentiments, of enviable intercourse, that she seeks to organize in and around herself. Yes, during these years when her life was complete and powerful, instinctively, and as a consequence of the sympathy and impetuous curiosity of her nature, she aspired,—and we say it in her praise,—she aspired to a vast court, to an empire increasing in intelligence and affection, where nothing gracious or important was omitted, where all degrees of talent, of birth, of patriotism, and of beauty, were enthroned under her own eyes: empress of thought, she loved to confine within the limits of her free dominion all the *appanages* of her state. When Bonaparte persecuted her, he was vaguely angry at that rivalry which, unconsciously to herself, she assumed.

The dominating charm in Mme. de Staël's character, the chief point in which all the contrasts of that character were united, the quick and penetrating faculty which, passing from one thing to another, supported that marvellous medley, was most certainly conversation, an impromptu eloquence, which sprang quick and sudden from the divine depths of her soul,—this, properly speaking, was what constituted for her *la vie*, a magical expression which she has used so often, and which, following her example, we must employ very often in speaking of her. Her contemporaries are all unanimous on this point; if you admire or are touched by some clever or brilliant pages of her books, it may always be said of her, as of the great Athenian orator: "Imagine how grand that would have sounded spoken in her own voice." Adversaries and critics, who so readily assume to themselves a superiority fit to contend against the pre-eminence of any individual who seems too great and perfect in their eyes, who take some already acknowledged work of talent and bring it into competition against the new claimant for honour, render on this point due homage to Mme. de Staël,—an interested homage, it may be, and even rather treacherous, but quite equal to that of her admirers. Fontanes, in 1800, ended the famous articles of the *Mercure* by these words: "In writing she still supposed herself to be conversing. All who heard her applauded. I had not heard her when I criticised her." For a very long time, indeed, Mme. de Staël's writings reflected the mannerisms of her conversational style. Reading her fluent and sparkling productions, one might almost believe one heard her voice. A slightly careless manner of sketching her subject, a flighty style quite allowable in conversation, but noticeable to a reader, alone forces one to observe a change in the mode of expression, which requires more conciseness. Still, superior as Mme. de Staël's conversation may have been to her writings, at least as far as her earlier works are concerned, we do not find her like some great debaters and orators, such as Mirabeau and Diderot, who, after the manner of Talma, powerful and famous though they were in their display of eloquence, have left us no written testimony at all equal to their influence and their glory; she, on the contrary, has left us plenty of enduring work to testify most worthily of her talent, and posterity has no need of borrowed explanations, nor of a long array of contemporaneous testimony in her favour. Perhaps,—and M. de Chateaubriand has remarked this in the judgment he pronounced on her about the time she died,—to make her works more perfect, it would be quite sufficient to deprive her of one of her talents, namely, conversation. However, just as we find her in reality, so she very beautifully accomplishes her task as an author. Despite some faults of style, M. de Chateaubriand has said in the same place, she will add one more to the list of names which can never die. Her writings, indeed, even with all their imperfections in point of detail, their quick, hurried glimpses, their looseness or want of continuity, often serve the better to interpret the rare conception of her impulsive, sensitive heart; *and then, as a work of poetic art, *Corinne* alone will stand as her immortal monument. In *Corinne*, Mme. de Staël displays artistic qualities of the highest order, while otherwise she will for ever be eminent in virtue of her talents as politician, moralist, critic, and writer of mémoires. It is this uniform yet varied life, the soul breathing through her writings, stirring about them, and the circumstances under which they were composed, which we would try to conjure up, in some places to concentrate, in order to convey to others the profound impression we ourselves have formed of them. We know how delicate a task it is to make this half-conjectural and altogether poetic impression accord with the still freshly remembered reality, how immediate contemporaries have always some peculiarity to oppose to the idea we desire to conceive of the person they have known; we also know, that in the arrangement of such a stormy, changeful life, there are many slips in the general design which distance of time adjusts; but this is rather a sketch than a biography, a reflex of moral portraiture in the form of a literary critique; and, moreover, I have tried, in describing the general characteristics of this noble-minded woman, to remember, and to take into consideration, many more minute details than it is possible to mention.

Mlle. Germain Necker, growing up betwixt the rather rigid severity of her mother, and the half-playful, half-encouraging criticism of her father, naturally was more influenced by the latter, and she early became an infant prodigy. She had her place in the salon, on a little wooden stool close to Mme. Necker's chair, who made her hold herself very straight and stiff; Mme. Necker, however, was unable to constrain the child's replies to the questions put to her by celebrities such as Grimm, Thomas, Rayñal, Gibbon, and Marmontel, who enjoyed crowding round her, provoking opinions from her, and never finding her at fault. Mme. Necker de Saussure has graphically described her wonderful powers, at this early age, in the excellent sketch of her cousin she has written. Mlle. Necker then read books much beyond her age, went to the play, and afterwards wrote down her recollections of it; when quite a child, her favourite game was to cut out paper figures of kings and queens and make them perform tragedies; these were her marionettes, as Goethe had his. The dramatic instinct, the craving for emotional sensation, was apparent in everything she did. When only eleven, Mlle. Necker wrote portraits and character studies, according to the fashion of the time. At fifteen, she had written extracts from the *L'Esprit des Lois*, with marginal notes; and at the same age, in 1781, after the publication of the *Compte-rendu*, she wrote an anonymous letter on the subject to her father, who, however, recognised his daughter's style of writing. But her ruling characteristic was that extreme sensibility, which, towards the end of the eighteenth century, and chiefly under the influence of Jean-Jacques, began to dominate youthful hearts — sensibility which afforded such a singular contrast to the excessive analysis and the incredulous pretension of the waning century. In that rather inordinate recoil upon the powerful instincts of nature, reverie, melancholy, pity, enthusiastic admiration of genius, virtue, and misfortune, the sentiments which *La Nouvelle Héloïse* had propagated, took a strong hold

of Mlle. Necker, and impressed all the first part of her
life and her work with a tone of ingenuous exaggeration,
which is not without its charm, even when it draws
forth a smile. This disposition was first manifested
in her enthusiastic admiration of her father, an enthusiasm which time and death only increased, but
which sprang up in these early years, and which at
certain moments almost took the form of jealousy of
her mother. In her life of M. Necker, when speaking of
the long time he spent in Paris when still young and
unmarried, she says: "Sometimes in his conversations
with me in his exile, he would describe to me that
period of his life, the thought of which moved me
deeply, that time when I could imagine him so young,
so loveable, so lonely! at an age when, if fate had made
us contemporaries, our destinies might have been
united for ever;" but she added: "My mother required
a husband who could not be compared with other men;
she found him, spent her life with him, and God
preserved her from the misfortune of outliving him . . .
she deserved happiness better than I did." This
adoration of Mme. de Staël for her father is, with more
solemnity and certainly not less depth, the inversion
and counterpart of the sentiment Mme. de Sévigné had
towards her daughter; it is refreshing to meet with
such pure and ardent affections in such brilliant minds.
As regards Mme. de Staël, one can account for the
warmth and continuity of her filial worship; in all the
disappointments of her life, in the gradual extinction of
all illusions of the heart and of the imagination, only
one human being, one alone among all this so beloved
of old, was for ever in her thoughts, a pure and stainless
love, which time never diminished; on that revered head
rested, immortal and already glorified, all the otherwise
vanished passion of her youth.

At that age of enthusiasm, romantic, dreaming love, and the obstacles it encountered, and fearlessness of suffering and death, were, next to her peculiar adoration of her father, the cherished sentiments of her heart, of that heart so quick and sensitive, *which even joy moved to tears*. She preferred to write on such subjects, and did so surreptitiously, as also by stealth she read certain books which Mme. Necker would have forbidden. I can almost see her in the study, under her mother's very eyes, walking up and down the room, a volume in her hand, reading the book she was obliged to read as she approached her mother's chair, and then, as she slowly walked away again, replacing it by a sentimental romance, perhaps some novel of Mme. Riccoboni's. In after years, she said that the abduction of Clarissa was one of the events of her youth,—an expression which sums up a whole world of first emotions; whether it be *àpropos* of Clarissa or of some other hero or heroine, every tender and poetic imagination ought to echo this.

The earliest printed work of Mlle. Necker's, if it was really hers, must have been a volume called *Letters from Nanine to Simphel*, which M. Beuchot seems to attribute to our authoress, but which was, in course of time (1818), disowned. This little romance, which treats of nothing unusual for an enthusiastic and innocent young girl to have imagined, and the plot of which scarcely differs from those of *Sophie*, of *Mirza*, or of *Pauline*, and other early productions, shows even greater inexperience as regards style and composition. I find nothing remarkable in it, either as regards the style of language or the rustic colouring, peculiar to a heroine of fourteen, except these words of Nanine: "I succeeded yesterday morning in going to the tomb; there I wept a torrent of tears, precious tears, which love and sorrow lend to unhappy people like me. A heavy shower which came on made me think that nature felt my grief. Each leaf seemed to weep with me; the birds were silenced by my sighs. This idea made such an impression on my soul, that I uttered aloud my earnest prayers to the Eternal Being. Unable to remain longer in that deserted place, I returned home to hide my sorrow," etc.

Sophie, or *Secret Sentiments*, written when Mme. de Staël was twenty, about 1786, or rather earlier, is a dramatic poem, the scene of which is laid in an English garden, shaded by cypress trees, and with a funereal urn in the distance. Cécile, a child of six, runs up to the melancholy Sophie, whom a silent passion devours, and addresses her thus :—

"Why then so far away from us do you remain?
My father is distressed.
Sophie. Your father?
Cécile. Yes, dearest ; he fears that you are melancholy.
Explain that word to me."

This was just how Mlle. Necker abruptly asked the old Maréchale de Mouchy, one day, what she thought of love;—a joke which M. Necker was fond of relating about his daughter, and which she was fond of recalling to his memory.

There was, even if not visible in her earlier writings, certainly, in Mme. de Staël's nature, a vivacity closely allied to sadness, a *spirituelle* petulance along with the melancholy, a piquant tendency to turn herself into ridicule, which saved her from the least approach to heaviness, and testified to the vigorous strength of her mind.

It is in that poem called *Sophie* that we find the charming lines which the author's personal friends still recall with pleasure : when heard for the first time, one marvels at not knowing them, asking where could

Mme. de Staël have said them,—no one dreams of finding that beautiful, half-buried pearl where it is.

> Mais un jour vous saurez ce qu'éprouve le cœur,
> Quand un vrai sentiment n'en fait pas le bonheur;
> Lorsque sur cette terre on se sent délaissée,
> Qu'on n'est d'aucun objet la première pensée;
> Lorsque l'on peut souffrir, sûr que ses douleurs
> D'aucun mortel jamais ne font couler les pleurs.
> On se désenterésse à la fin de soi même,
> On cesse de s'aimer, si quelqu'un ne nous aime;
> Et d'insipides jours, l'un sur l'autre entassés,
> Se passent lentement et sont vite effacés.*
>
> Acte II. Scene viii.

The three novels published in 1795, although written ten years earlier,—*Mirza, Adélaïde and Théodore, Pauline,*—are exactly in the same style as *Sophie*, and their easy prose makes them more attractive. They are invariably (whether the scene is laid among African savages or in the depths of an English forest) about unfortunate people enveloped in a cloud of sentimental misery, lovers reduced to shadows by the disastrous tidings of infidelity, or there is a tomb half buried among trees. As I read of these blighted hopes and untimely deaths, I think of the good Abbé Prevost and his very similar characters; or, more correctly speaking, I find myself really walking in the woods of Saint-Ouen, where

---

* Perhaps you soon will know the aching of a heart,
When even noble thoughts no happiness impart;
When in this world we feel ourselves forsaken,
And of our woes no tender heed is taken;
When one must suffer, certain that one's grief
From friendship's tears will find no sweet relief:
And so, at length, of one's sad lot made weary,
Beloved by none, and palled by life so dreary,
The dull, insipid days pass one by one;
And time's slow sands to quick oblivion run.—TR.

Mlle. Necker dreamed, or in the gardens of Ermenonville, where her many pilgrimages brought inspiration. I know under which shady alley one heroine strolled, from which leafy avenue another rushed in tears. Yet the time spent here must have been very short, and in her early youth. Later,—still quite soon enough,—stricken by the spectacle of public passion, perhaps also warned by some wound, she would experience a reaction against that development of extreme sensibility of which she was conscious. In her book on *The Influence of the Passions*, she tries to combat them, she would suppress them ; but even her accusing accents are full of it still, and that forced tone only appears the more passionate. However great the tendency to stoicism may appear to be in *Delphine*, she will for ever remain the most bewitching genius of love.

M. de Guibert wrote a sketch of Mlle. Necker just as she reached her twentieth year, a brilliant portrait, quoted by Mme. Necker de Saussure. The study is said to be borrowed from a Greek poet, and very aptly expresses the prevailing taste of society at that time ; it is known that the portraits of the Duke and Duchess de Choiseul were written by the Abbé Barthélemy under the names of Arsame and Phédime. Here are a few of the characteristics of M. de Guibert's Zulmé : " Zulmé is only twenty years old, but she is already one of the most honoured priestesses of Apollo ; it is she whose incense is most pleasant to him, and whose voice he prefers to any other. . . . Her great black eyes sparkle with the light of genius ; her ebony locks fall in rich profusion on her shoulders ; her features are more marked than gentle, there is something in them which promises more than the usual fate of her sex." I have myself seen a portrait * of Mlle. Necker

* Portrait by Rehberg.—TR.

in her youth, which comfirms this description. She had wavy hair, a clear and frank expression, a high forehead, and lips apart as if about to speak, the blushing cheeks spoke of quick and sensitive feelings; the neck and arms were bare, her dress gathered together in loose folds by a sash. This picture might be the Sophie in *Emile*, the author of the *Lettres sur Jean-Jacques* accompanying her admirable guide in his Elysian fields, pleased with all his efforts, at one time following in his footsteps, at another going on before.

The *Lettres sur Jean-Jacques*, written in 1787, really form the first of Mme. de Staël's serious works, the production in which she makes it apparent that her intellectual inclinations are already armed with the eloquence and solidity till then only vaguely tried. Grimm, in his Correspondence, gives extracts from this charming work, as he calls it, of which there were only twenty copies printed at first, yet notwithstanding the cautious reserve maintained in its distribution, it did not long escape the honour of a public edition. Before giving any extracts from the book, the gifted *habitué* of Mme. Necker's salon bestows much praise on the authoress, describing her as "this young lady, surrounded by all the illusions of her age, all the pleasures of the city and of the court, all the homage which her own celebrity and her father's fame brought her, all this without taking into account her desire to please, which of itself would probably have been as effective as all the accessories which nature and art have lavished on her." The *Letters on Jean-Jacques* are her grateful homage to the admired and favourite author, to him with whom Mme. de Staël had so much in common. Many writers are careful to keep silent about, or else they criticise, the literary parents from whom they spring: it shows a noble candour to appear in public for the first time acknowledging and glorifying him to whom we owe our inspiration, from whom to us has flowed that broad stream of beautiful language, for which in olden times Dante rendered thanks to Virgil; thus also, in her literary life, Mme. de Staël displays her filial passion. The *Letters on Jean-Jacques* are a poem, but a poem nurtured on grave thoughts, while at the same time varied by delicate observations, a poem with the bold, sustained rhythm recognisable in Corinne as she descends the steps of the Capitol. All the future works of Mme. de Staël of every description, whether romantic or political, or relating to social morality, are shadowed in the rapid, harmonious eloquence of that eulogy of Rousseau's work, just as a great musical composition manifests all the latent depth of its conception in the overture. The success of these Letters, which corresponded with the sympathetic impulses of the time, was immense and universal.

Grimm agrees with this (but according to a communicated manuscript), and gives an extract from the *Éloge de M. de Guibert* (1789), since printed in the complete edition of the works. Mme. de Staël's admiration for the object of this *Éloge* is not less enthusiastic than it had been immediately before for *Jean - Jacques*, although in the latter case the sentiment may seem less impartial; but in this work she has propagated new and daring political views, and is too lavish in her persuasive deification of and belief in genius. Through all the exaggerated pathos with which she pleads the cause of moderation, she yet succeeds in enlisting our pity and esteem for that distinguished man, so much admired and envied in his time, though quite forgotten since, and who henceforth will be remembered only through her. M. de Guibert, in his discourse on his admission to the Academy, very often used the word *glory*, thus

involuntarily betraying, she says, his majestic spirit.
For my own part, I have to thank that nobly ambitious
and misunderstood man of genius for my earliest
comprehension of the means and ideas of reform, of
the States-General, and of a force of citizen soldiers,
but I render him special thanks for having, with such
sure and certain confidence, foretold the coming greatness of *Corinne*.

Worldly honour and literary fame brought upon
Mme. de Staël about this time the impertinent banter
of the wits, just as, a little later, in 1800, we again find
them in league against her. Champcenetz and Rivarol,
who, in 1788, had published the *Petit Dictionnaire des
Grands Hommes*, compiled two years later another *Petit
Dictionnaire des Grands Hommes de la Révolution*, which
they solemnly dedicated to the *Baroness de Staël,
Ambassadress from Sweden to the Nation.*" This pamphlet
gave the tone to the criticisms which were subsequently
circulated against her. Rivarol and Champcenetz possessed, indeed, the same wonderful faculty for irony and
caricature, which Fiévée, Michaud, and others afterwards displayed against Mme. de Staël. But by this
time, as Grimm says, the object of those attacks had
gained such celebrity that criticisms of such a nature
were harmless. The terrible events of the French
Revolution occurred to cut short that first part of a
literary life, so brilliantly inaugurated, and to suspend,
usefully, I believe, for thought, the whirl of worldly
pleasures, which gave no respite.

Notwithstanding her absolute faith in M. Necker,
her complete adoption of his views, and the detailed
vindication of his political opinions which she sets
forth in her book of *Reflections on the French Revolution*,
it must be remembered that Mme. de Staël, in her youth
and enthusiasm, at that time ventured even further than

he did in the same theories. She did not agree with the complications of the English constitution; and on many points she was more advanced than even the constitutional royalists of that enlightened generation, Narbonne, Montmorency, or even La Fayette himself.

Indeed, if from this date it is necessary to assign a particular line of politics to a judgment so swayed by sentiment, we should be more correct to say that Mme. de Staël was influenced rather by the constitutional royalists of '91, than by the group composed of MM. Malouet, Monnier, and Necker. We find, besides, in a journalistic article of hers which has been preserved, the only written expression of her opinions at this epoch; she there, under the immediate impression of his loss, extols the departed Mirabeau, a favourable judgment which, however, she afterwards retracts.

Mme. de Staël left Paris, though not without some danger and difficulty, after the 2nd of September. She spent the year of Terror in the department of Vaud, with her father and some refugee friends, M. de Montmorency and M. de Jaucourt.

From the terrace gardens of Coppet, on the banks of the Lake of Geneva, her thoughts were chiefly occupied in comparing the glorious sunshine and the peaceful beauty of nature with the horrors everywhere perpetrated by the hand of man. Excepting her eloquent cry of pity for the queen,* and the poem on *Misfortune*, her genius observed a scrupulous silence: like the regular stroke of the oars on the surface of the lake, there came from afar the hollow echo of the axe upon the scaffold.

The condition of agonized depression in which Mme. de Staël existed during these terrible months, left her, in the intervals of her devoted exertions for others, no desire for herself but death, a longing for the end of

* *The Defence of the Queen*, published in 1793.—Tr.

the world, and of that human race which could permit such horrors. "I would," she says, "have made even thought a reproach to myself, because it was separate from sorrow." The 9th Thermidor gave her back that faculty of thought more energetic after its paralysis, and the use she promptly put it to was the composition of her *Reflections upon Peace*, the first part addressed to Pitt, and the second to the French. As a display of profound commiseration and of calm justice, and as an appeal to opinion not lost in fanaticism, to forget the past, to seek conciliation, and as an expression of apprehension of the evils born of extremes, this latter contains sentiments at once opportune and generous, and indicates elevation of soul and of ideas. There is an attitude of ancient inspiration in that youthful womanly figure springing up and standing on the still smoking ashes to exhort a nation. There is, moreover, great political wisdom, and a thorough understanding of the real situation in the prematurely wise counsel which her passionate accents unfold. As an eyewitness of the daring success of fanaticism, Mme. de Staël declares it to be one of the most formidable of human weapons; she considers it an inevitable element in every struggle, and in times of revolution necessary for victory, but she now desires to restrict it to her own personal circle. Since fanaticism inclines towards that republican form which it at last attained, she invites all who are wise, all friends of honest liberty, whatever views they may hold, to join together sincerely in that new membership; she solemnly implores the bleeding hearts not to rise against an accomplished fact. "It seems to me," she says, "that vengeance (even if it is necessary in irreparable afflictions) cannot bind itself to any particular form of government, cannot make those political shocks desirable which affect the innocent as well as the guilty." According to her, there is no period of a revolution more critical, more opportune for intelligent effort and sacrifice, than when fanaticism seeks to make popular the establishment of a government purely democratic, and without *prestige*—if by any new misfortune, sober minds should lend their consent to it. We perceive that she treats fanaticism entirely as a physical power, as she would speak of weight, a grand proof that her mind rose superior to disaster. Convinced that action is the result of diverse opinions, we find Mme. de Staël, in this work, strenuously endeavouring to convince the French in her own rank, the old constitutional royalists, of the necessity for freely rallying round the established order, so that they may bias temperately without attempting to flatter. She says to them: "To oppose yourselves to an experience as novel as was that of the republic in France, when there were so many chances against its success, so many evils to endure in order to obtain it, is a very different thing from trying by another kind of presumption to make as much blood flow as has already been spilt, so that you may recover the only government you consider possible, namely, monarchy."

We feel that such conclusions must have appeared too republican to many among those to whom she addressed herself; they must also have seemed weak to the pure conventionalists, and to those who were republican from conviction. In her other works, published up to 1803, we find Mme. de Staël becoming more and more attached to that form of government, and to those essential conditions which alone can maintain it. Most of the philosophical principles which helped in their development under the well-composed and much-respected constitution of the year

III., had in her a brilliant mouthpiece, during that ill-appreciated period of her political and literary life. It was not till later, and more especially towards the latter years of the Empire, that the notion of the English constitution seized upon her imagination.

In the volume of short pieces which Mme. de Staël published in 1795, we find, besides three stories which date from her girlhood, a charming *Essay on Fiction*, of more recent date, and a little poem, called *Misfortune*, or *Adèle and Edouard*, written while under the influence of the Terror. It is remarkable that at such a time, when all her usual talents were, as it were, suspended or crushed, the art of song, of poetry, should have visited her, coming as a comfort and occupation; and this manifests the wonderful power of poetry to soothe even the most secret grief, of which it is the instinctive plaint, the melodious sigh which nature craves, a language of surpassing sweetness, in which, when other language fails, we can still pour out our sorrows. But in this poetic romance, as in every attempt of this description, intention with Mme. de Staël is better than result; sentiment prevails,—is, as we have already indicated, its chief aim,—but she exclaims:

> "Souvent les yeux fixés sur ce beau paysage
> Dont le lac avec pompe agrandit les tableaux,
> Je contemplais ces monts qui, formant son rivage,
> Peignent leur cime auguste au milieu de ses eaux:
> Quoi! disais-je, ce calme où se plait la nature
> Ne peut-il pénétrer dans mon cœur agité ?
> Et l'homme seul, en proie aux peines qu'il endure,
> De l'ordre général serait-il excepté."*

---

* Often when my eyes rest on that beautiful landscape, which the lake reflects in all its grandeur, I contemplate those mountains, which, rising from its banks, paint their summits in the midst of its waters: Why! I ask, can this calm which nature

This conception of the discord between a glorious smiling nature and human suffering and death, has inspired most of the poets of modern time to express themselves in accents of bitterness or melancholy: Byron, in the powerfully satirical introduction to the second canto of *Lara* ("But mighty nature bounds as from her birth"); Shelley, in the strained and painful ending of *Alastor* (". . . And mighty Earth, from sea and mountain, city and wilderness," etc.); M. de Lamartine, in the *Dernier Pèlerinage de Childe Harold* ("Triomphe, disait-il, immortelle Nature," etc.); and M. Hugo, in one of the *sunsets* of his *Feuilles d'Automne:*

"Je m'en irai bientôt au milieu de la Fête,
Sans que rien manque au Monde immense et radieux."

Has not Corinne herself, on Cape Misenc, uttered these nobly inspired words, "O Earth! all bathed in blood and tears, thou hast never ceased to bring forth fruit and flowers! Art thou, then, pitiless towards man? when his dust returns to thy bosom, dost thou not thrill and tremble?" Now, how is it that a poet at heart, as this poetic expression undoubtedly proves Mme. de Staël to have been, yet renders her profound sentiment in prose? Does it mean, as Mme. Necker de Saussure explains, that the structure of poetry was an art so perfected in France, that the labour it involved to one not early accustomed to it, quenched the poetic spirit? Or does it mean, as a less indulgent critic has conjectured, that being seldom able to subject herself, even in her prose, to strict rules, Mme. de Staël was probably less fit than any of her contemporaries to yield herself gracefully to the bondage of rhyme.

so delights in, not penetrate to my restless heart? Is man only a prey to the torments which he bears, is he alone to be exempt from nature's rule?—TR.

Besides, we find many eminent writers severely correct, accomplished, and artistic in their prose, who are yet unable, in consequence of that new individuality of style, to express themselves skilfully and fluently in verse. And again, does not one of our greatest and most melodious poets offer us the singular example of intentional carelessness, in his poetry as well as in his prose writings? It is better, therefore, to recognise, that quite independently of either natural or acquired style, poetry is a gift, like singing. Those whom the Muse has destined to reach her beauteous realms, arrive there as if on wings. With Mme. de Staël, as with Benjamin Constant, attempts of this kind were indifferent. Thought, which with both is unconstrained and distinguished in prose composition, does not spontaneously lend itself to the winged flight of poetry, which to be properly conceived ought to take form with the birth of the thought.

All Mme. de Staël's faculties were kept in constant activity by the storms through which her impetuous nature passed, and in every sense she made a rapid flight. Her imagination, her delicate sensibility, her penetrating power of analysis and judgment, mingled, united, and contributed all together in the production of celebrated works. When the *Essay on Fictions* was composed, it already included all the poetry of *Delphine*. Wounded by the spectacle of reality, Mme. de Staël's imagination is touched, and she yearns to create things happier and better; troubles, even the remembrance of which, or, at least, the story of them, will cause our softest tears to flow. But, at the same time, every one of Mme. de Staël's fictions, besides containing genuine, natural romance, manifests her power of analyzing the workings of human passion; this is her aim, and it is a purpose destitute of mythological, or allegorical, or supernatural conceit, or of any philosophical intention beyond the depth of ordinary readers.

Clémentine, Clarisse, Julie, Werther, are the witnesses she quotes to prove the infinite power of love,—"beloved comforters," she calls them,—and from the emotion which the mention of their names inspires, it is easy to foresee that a sister will very soon be born to them. A note to this essay mentions, in terms of praise, *L'Esprit des Religions*, a work begun about this time by Benjamin Constant, though not published till thirty years later. Mme. de Staël became acquainted with the author for the first time in Switzerland, about September 1794; she had read several chapters of this book, which, let us remark in passing, was in its first draft more philosophic, and much more in accord with the issues of the analysis of the eighteenth century, than it afterwards grew to. The *Essay on Fictions*, with its rapid fancies, gives us even at that time admired, intense, and profound ideas, those delicious touches of sentiment peculiar to Mme. de Staël, which, properly speaking, form a poetry which is hers alone, her own dreamy melody; as she utters them, there seem to be tears in the very accents of her thrilling voice. Yet they are mere nothings, it is the tone alone which strikes us; as, for example: *Dans cette vie qu'il faut passer plutôt que sentir*, etc. *Il n'y a sur cette terre que des commencements.* . . . And this thought, so applicable to her own works, "Yes, it is true, the book which provides even a day's distraction from grief, is useful to the best of men."

But this style of sentimental inspiration, this mysterious reflection from the depths of the heart, illumines all her book on the *Influence of the Passions*, giving it an indescribable charm, which, to certain melancholy natures, and at a certain time of life, is surpassed by no

E

other literature, neither by the sadness of Ossian nor the gloom of Oberman. Besides this, the first part of the book is very remarkable from a political point of view. The author, who has indeed discussed in full only the influence of the passions on the happiness of individuals, designed in the second part to try to examine as to the influence of the same motives on the welfare of societies, and the principal questions which prognosticated that wide research are approached in an eloquent introduction. In the beginning, held in check by memories of that terrible past which still pursued her, Mme. de Staël exclaims that she does not wish her thoughts to dwell on it. "At that dread picture every throb of anguish is revived; one shudders, and hot anger burns; we would fight and die." Coming generations may be able calmly to study these last two years, but for her it is impossible; she does not wish to reason about them, therefore she turns to the future; she separates generous ideas from evil men, and clears certain principles from the crimes with which they have been soiled; she still hopes. Her judgment on the English constitution is explicit; she believes that henceforth in France we might be satisfied with some fictions hallowed by that aristocratic establishment of our neighbours. She is not in favour of the antagonistic equilibrium of powers, but of their co-operation in one uniform direction, through different rates of progress. In all sciences, she says, we begin by the most compound in order to arrive at the simplest; in mechanics, we had the water-wheels of Marly before pumps came into use. "Without attempting to turn a comparison into a proof, perhaps," she adds, "when, a hundred years ago, in England, the idea of liberty again dawned, the combined organization of the English government was at the highest point of perfection it could then attain; but to-day, after the Revolution, we in France, from a simpler basis, can show results similar in some respects and superior in others." France, then, from her own showing, ought to profit from this grand experience, the misery of which lies in the past and the hope in the future. "Allow us," she says to Europe,—"allow us in France to fight, conquer, suffer, die, in our affections, in our most cherished traditions, to be born again, it may be, afterwards for the wondering admiration of the world! . . . Are you not glad that a whole nation should place itself in the foremost rank of civilisation to bear the brunt of all prejudices, to try all principles?" Marie-Joseph Chénier ought to have called to remembrance many passages inspired by the generous and free spirit of these hopeful years, rather than attack our author, as in his *Tableau de la Littérature*, he has done, for a dubious expression which escaped her in regard to Condorcet. Towards the end of the introduction, Mme. de Staël speaks again of the influence of individual passion, that science of mental happiness, that is to say, *of the least possible misery*, and she finishes in language of touching eloquence. The craving for devotion and development, the pity to which the experience of grief gives birth, the forethought and the anxiety to comfort, if possible, the trials of one and of all; as one might express it, the motherly compassion of genius for all unfortunate humanity, are very striking in these pages; they overflow in words, the tone and accent of which cannot be qualified. Nowhere so distinctly as in these admirable pages, does Mme. de Staël manifest herself to be, what she will remain for all time—a cordial, kindly genius. In her writings, her conversation, and in herself personally, there was a healthy, soothing emotion, which those who came in contact with her experienced, which still survives, and will unfold itself to those who read her works. Very different are such lofty geniuses, male or female, as Lara or Lélia (I speak of Lélia only, and not of you, O Geneviève! O Lavinia !)* In Mme. de Staël, we find nothing arrogant or satirical against poor humanity. Notwithstanding her *penchant* for matchless symbols, which everywhere come flashing out in her romances, she believed in the equality of the human family: Mme. Necker de Saussure tells us that, even as regards the intellectual faculties, the very small original proportion of superior talent, which the most eminent men possess over the average generality of mankind, is of little real importance. But, whether from theory or not, her natural impulse was not stayed; her impressive voice appeals first to all the good qualities within us, rouses them, and puts new life into them. Her intention is always sociable, her words always conciliatory, influencing us to love our fellows. In this book, *The Influence of the Passions*, she has expressed many ideas which are also to be found in the *Considérations sur la Révolution française* of M. de Maistre, written and published precisely at the same time; but what a different tone! The scornful aristocrat, with his hard, paradoxical orthodoxy, likes to set forth to contemporaries and victims their *posterity, who will dance upon their tombs;* his powerful intellect judges calmly, and with offensive rigidity. Mme. de Staël, through some illusive vapours, frequently penetrates into the future as deeply as M. de Maistre, but with the spirit of one who feels her own part in it. I shall not

* In studying George Sand, I applied myself betimes to discern the delicacy and pathos which I desired to see triumphing over the passionate element and the bombastic style. As the years passed, this great genius, without growing weak, became much more refined.

analyze the book: let any one re-peruse the chapter on *Love;* it is the story of her heart, a throbbing yet half-veiled heart, which has beat for thirty years, and it is enough to let us know her. We can hear all round her there the echoes of a thousand thoughts which will nevermore be forgotten. One little passage among many others which I often repeat, is in my memory: *The life of the soul is more active when on the throne of a Cæsar.* If I linger too long on these older writings of Mme. de Staël's, on this book, *The Influence of the Passions,* and presently on that on *Literature,* it is because through them she first became known to me; because I have read them, especially *Influence,* not at five-and-twenty, as she advises, but earlier, at that time of life when all is severe simplicity in politics as in love, and full of solemn resolves; when, believing oneself the most unfortunate of beings, we ardently dream of the progress and felicity of the world; at that age, which we ever more and more regret, when the violence of confused hopes and disturbing passions hides itself under a stoicism which we think will last for ever, under the influence of which we could renounce everything, because we are on the threshold of feeling everything. Even now, these two works of Mme. de Staël's, *The Influence of the Passions* and the book on *Literature,* seem to me illustrious productions, altogether peculiar to an epoch which was in its glory during the time of the Directorate, or, as we may better express it, of the constitution of the year III. They could not have been written before; nor could they have been written afterwards, under the Empire. They present to me, with an appearance of inexperience, the poetry, and the exalted, enthusiastic, and pure philosophy, of that republican period, the literary counterpart of such a march as that of Moreau over the Rhine, or of some early Italian battlefield. M. de Chateaubriand, and all the reactionary movement of 1800, had not yet begun hostilities; Mme. de Staël alone propagated sentiment and poetic spiritualism, but in the midst of the philosophy of the century.

Her book, *The Influence of the Passions*, was favourably received : the *Mercury*, not yet revived as it was in 1800, gave extracts from it, accompanied by kindly criticisms. Mme. de Staël had returned to Paris after 1795, and up to the period of her exile she continued to make long and frequent sojourns there. We do not require to enter into details as to her political conduct, the chief lines of which she has sketched in her *Considérations sur la Révolution française*, and it would be rather uncertain to try to supplement with particulars from equivocal sources what she has not told us herself. But in a very discriminating and very clever article on Benjamin Constant, which the *Revue des Deux-Mondes* has published, we are given an idea of Mme. de Staël and of her then existing connections which is quite incorrect, although consistent with general prejudice, and which for these reasons we cannot help correcting. Mme. de Staël's salon in Paris is represented as the rendezvous of a *côterie* of discontented, *blasé* men, belonging both to the old and new *régime*, quite incongruous in a pure republic, and hostile to that honest establishment which was being so vainly attempted. By way of contrast, Benjamin Constant is made to appear as an ingenuous novice, inclined sentimentally towards moderate republicanism, and in sympathy with these same *patriotes*, who in Mme. de Staël's salon are described to him as bloodthirsty monsters. Correct and careful in his handling of Benjamin Constant's politics, the ingenious writer has not rendered equal justice to Mme. de Staël. Whatever may have been, indeed, the unavoidable mixture in her salon, as in all salons of that motley period, her wishes were most manifestly in favour of the honourable and reasonable, relative to the establishment of the year III.

Without paying too much heed to the opinion she expresses thereupon in the *Considérations*, which might possibly be suspected of after-rearrangement, we require no further proof than her writings from 1795 to 1800, and the visible results of her actions. As a rule, there are two sorts of people whom it is unnecessary to consult or believe either in regard to Mme. de Staël's connections, or the part she herself played at this period: on one side, the royalists, firmly adhering to their old malice against her, accused her of absurd confederacies, of Jacobin tendencies, indeed, of adherence to the 18th Fructidor, and of I know not what; on the other side, there were those whose evidence on the subject we ought not to challenge, the Conventionnels, more or less ardent, who, themselves favourable to the 18th Fructidor, and afterwards adherents of the 18th Brumaire, finally served under the Empire,—they had never met this independent woman except in the ranks of the opposition. The truest political friends of Mme. de Staël at this time are to be found in the enlightened and moderate group in which we distinguish Lanjuinais, Boissy-d'Anglas, Cabanis, Garat, Daunou, Tracy, and Chénier. She esteemed them, and courted their society; the bond of friendship which united her to some among them was very strong. After the 18th Brumaire, keener interests bound them to each other; the opposition of Benjamin Constant to the Tribunat was the last and strongest link.

When the book on *Literature* and *Delphine* appeared, it was, as we shall see, only in that tribe of political friends that she found zealous defenders against the spite and fury of the opposite party. And now, allow me to say at once, it is never my intention to make Mme. de Staël out to be more cautious in thought, more circumspect in regard to her friendships,* or more exclusive, than she really was. She has always been quite the contrary of *exclusive*. As her bold young reason declared itself for that republican cause, her wit and her tastes had a thousand sympathies with opinions and sentiments of different origin, of a nature either more frivolous or more delicate, but profoundly distinct; it is one of her weaknesses, though redounding to her honour, that she was able thus to reconcile contrasts. If Garat, Cabanis, Chénier, Ginguené, Daunou, dined together at her house once a week, or rather, once a *décade* (as it was still usual to say), the other nine days were devoted to other friends, other social customs, other shades of sentiment, which never intruded upon those graver friends. All this, I can well believe, was arranged by her with a certain degree of order, of authority, perhaps: M. de Montmorency, or any member of his set, was never by any chance to be met at her house on the day that the writers of the

* An English poet and moralist, William Cowper, who is in turn kindly and austere, although in speaking of France he is at times severe almost to the extent of injustice, is not altogether wrong when he describes the French (at the time of the American War) as that nation of a restless, meddling disposition, which interferes with everything—at least, with most things. Mme. de Staël could not help being even more French than most of her compatriots. It therefore often happened that her eagerness for development, her penetration, astonished people in England and Holland; eminent men of those reserved and prudent races were surprised when they met her for the first time in society. (See p. 88 of the book entitled *Notice et Souvenirs Biographiques de Comte Van Der Duyn*, etc., collected and published by the Baron de Grovestins, 1852.)

Décade philosophique met there to dine. Ginguené sometimes remarked this when leaving, and did not seem to be too well pleased at this very particular drawing of the line, which, in his opinion, was rather suggestive of aristocratic exclusiveness. His companions soon, however, soothed him into tolerance; while Mme. de Staël's high-bred amiability and courteous gravity charmed all.

The book on *Literature considered in connection with Social Institutions*, appeared in 1800, about a year before that other glorious and rival publication, which was already announced under the title of *Beauties Moral and Poetic of the Christian Religion*. Although the book on *Literature* may not since have had the direct effect or the influence which might have been expected, its appearance was at the time a great event in intellectual circles, and it raised very violent discussion. We shall try to review it, and to reanimate some of the actors in the work, to call them up from those vast cemeteries called *journals*, where they lie nameless.

We have frequently remarked upon the striking difference which exists between the advanced political principles of certain men, and the principles they obstinately adhere to in literature. The liberals and republicans have always scrupulously displayed classic taste in their literary theories, and it is from the other side that the brilliantly successful poetic innovation has chiefly come. The book on *Literature* was destined to precede this grievous inconsistency, and the intellect which inspired it would certainly have borne fruit in all directions, if the institutions of political liberty necessary to natural development had not been suddenly torn asunder, with all the ideas, moral and literary, which resulted therefrom. In a word, the younger generations, if they had had time to grow up under a government either honestly directorial, or moderately consular, might have been able to develop in themselves an inventive, poetic, sentimental inspiration, which would have harmonized with the results of modern philosophy and enlightenment, even had there been no literary advance except that catholic, monarchical, and chivalric reaction, which has divided the noblest faculties in all modern thought—a divorce which has not yet ceased.

The idea which Mme. de Staël never loses sight of in this work is the spirit of modern progress ; each advance she makes, each success, each hope, is for the undefined perfectibility of the human race. This idea, the germ of which we find in Bacon when he says, *Antiquitas sœculi juventus mundi;* which M. Leroux (*Revue Encyclopédique,* March 1833) has explicitly demonstrated as existing in the seventeenth century, by quoting more than one passage from Fontenelle and Perrault ; and which the eighteenth has propagated in all senses, till Turgot, who made it the subject of his Latin discourse at the Sorbonne, or Condorcet, who preached most enthusiastic Lenten discourses on it,— this idea animated and directed all Mme. de Staël's energies. "I do not think," she says, "that this great working out of the moral nature has ever been relinquished ; during the epochs of enlightenment, as in the dark ages, the gradual progress of the human intellect has never been interrupted." And again she says : "In studying history, it appears to me that one acquires the conviction that all the principal events tend to the same end, universal civilisation. . . . With all my faculties I adopt this philosophical belief : its chief advantage is that it inspires to noble sentiments." Mme. de Staël did not subject to the law of perfectibility the fine arts, those at least which belong more

particularly to the imagination; but she believes in
the progress of the sciences, and especially philosophy
and history, also to a certain extent poetry, which,
being among all the arts the one which depends more
directly on the imagination, admits in its modern
expression of an accent of deeper thoughtful melancholy, and an analysis of the passions unknown to
the older poets: from this point of view she declares
her predilection for Ossian and Werther, for the
Héloïse of Pope, Rousseau's Julie, and Aménaïde in
Tancrède. Her numerous allusions to Greek literature,
not very trustworthy in consequence of the levity with
which the subject is treated, and the paucity of detail,
still tend to give a general idea, which remains correct
in spite of the mistakes and deficiencies. The imposing, positive, and eloquently philosophic character
of the Latin literature we find firmly traced : and we
feel that in order to write of it she must have studied
Sallust and Cicero, and that she is conscious of existing
or possible similarities with her own epoch, with the
heroic genius of France. The influence of Christianity
on society at the time when the invading Barbarians
mixed with the degenerate Romans, is not altogether
ignored; but this appreciative homage is never in-
consistent with philosophy. A new and fertile idea,
which is very strongly urged in these later days,
developed by the Saint-Simonism, and other influences,
belongs, properly speaking, to Mme. de Staël; namely,
that the French Revolution having caused a veritable
invasion of Barbarians (into the domestic relations of
society), the question then arose of civilising and
blending the still rather rude issue of this invasion,
under a law of liberty and equality. At this present
time it is easy to perfect this idea : in 1789 it was the
bourgeoisie alone who invaded; the people of the

lowest ranks who forced the breach in 1793, have been several times driven back since then, while the *bourgeoisie* have vigorously maintained their position. At this present time there is a pause in the invasion as in the time of the Emperor Probus, or some similar hero. New invasions threaten, however; and it has yet to be discovered if they can be directed and controlled amicably, or if it is impossible to evade the path of violence. In either case the consequent intermingling must at last blend and co-operate. Now, it was Christianity that influenced that combined mass of Barbarians and Romans: where is the new Christianity which will in our day render the same moral service?

"Happy would it be," exclaims Mme. de Staël, "if we could find, as at the period of the invasion of the northern nations, a philosophical system, a virtuous enthusiasm, a strong and just legislation, which would be as the Christian religion has been, the sentiment in which conquerors and conquered could unite!"

At a later time, with advancing years, and less faith, as we shall see, either in new devices or in unlimited human power, Mme. de Staël would have trusted in nothing beyond the ancient and unique Christian religion for the means of moral regeneration which her prayerful cry invokes. But the way in which Christianity will set to work to regain its hold upon the society of the future, remains yet veiled; and for the most religious thinking minds, anxious consideration of this great problem is undiminished.

As soon as the book on *Literature* appeared, the *Décade Philosophique* published three articles or extracts, unsigned and uninitialed, giving a very exact and detailed analysis, with critical remarks and arguments, in which praise and justice were equally distributed.

The writer of these articles remarked that Ossian is but an imperfect type of the poetry of the north, and that the honour of representing northern poetry belongs by right to Shakespeare. *Apropos* of Homer's poems, we also read this passage, which points to a writer familiar with the various systems: "Mme. de Staël admits, without any possibility of doubt or discussion, that these poems are the work of one man, and belong to an earlier date than any other Greek poem. These facts have often been disputed, and one of the considerations which point to the possibility of their being disputed again, is the difficulty one has of reconciling them with several well-established facts of the history of human knowledge." The critic considers the book defective in plan and in method. He adds: "Another objection is the extreme subtlety in the combination of certain ideas. In some cases clear and well-recognised general facts are explained in a manner which is too far-fetched to be probable, and too minute to be in proportion to the ascertained results." But the power and originality he praises highly. "These two qualities," he says, "are all the more pleasing because we feel that they proceed from a delicate and deep sensibility, desirous of discovering in objects their analogy to the highest intellectual ideas, and to the noblest sentiments of the soul."

In the *Clef du Cabinet des Souverains*, a miscellaneous periodical published by Panckoucke, some *Observations* on the work of Mme. de Staël appeared from the pen of the learned doctor, Roussel, author of the book on *Woman*, but chiefly a criticism of Daunou, or at least a favourable analysis, cleverly accurate, with the criticisms hinted at rather than expressed, in the discreet style of this learned author, whose judgment carried so much weight, and who has a reputation for calm excellence in all he writes.* The *Journal des Débats* (11 Messidor, year VIII.) accepted, though somewhat curtailing it, a friendly article by M. Hochet. Three days later, as if recovered from this unexpected event, it published, under the title of "Variétés," an article, unsigned, in which, without naming Mme. de Staël, the system of perfectibility, and the disastrous consequences with which it is credited, are forcibly, even violently opposed. It said: "The genius which now presides over the destinies of France is a genius of wisdom, which has before its eyes the experience of centuries, as well as that of the Revolution. It does not lose itself in vain theories, nor is it ambitious of the glory of systems; it knows that men have always been the same, that their nature will never change; and it seeks in the past lessons wherewith to regulate the present. . . . It does not incline to throw us into fresh troubles by trying new experiments, by following up the shadow of a perfection which in the present day one tries to oppose to that which exists, and which may greatly favour the schemes of factionists, etc."

But on the subject of Mme. de Staël, the most celebrated articles of the day were the two extracts from Fontanes in the *Mercure de France*.

The monarchical, religious, and literary reaction of 1800 was indeed represented in every subject, and was displayed in all directions. Bonaparte looked favourably upon this movement, because he would necessarily profit by it, and the agitators in this progress kept on good terms with Bonaparte, who was not opposed to them. The *Journal des Debats* solemnly re-established literary criticism, and declared in an article by Geoffroy

* The letter of thanks which Mme. de Staël wrote to him may be read at page 94 of the *Documents Biographiques sur Daunou*, by M. Taillandier.

(30 Prairial, year VIII.), that "the extinction of factions, public tranquillity established on solid foundations, and a strong, wise, and moderate government, had at length given the French nation leisure to recover itself, and to collect its ideas." Dussault, Feletz, Delalot, Fiévée, Saint-Victor, and the Abbé of Boulogne, wrote frequently in this journal. *Le Mercure de France* had been revived, or rather reproduced, and it was in the first number of this re-publication that the first article by Fontanes against Mme. de Staël appeared. The other contributors to it were La Harpe, the Abbé of Vauxcelles, Gueneau de Mussy, M. de Bonald, M. de Chateaubriand, and several of the writers to the *Débats*. Each member of the *Mercure* was announced with loud praises by its daily auxiliary, which gave long extracts from it. The Lycée in the Rue de Valois had been opened again, and La Harpe delivered * there his brilliant, earnest recantations on the eighteenth century and against the Revolution, which the *Débats* of the next day, and the *Mercure* that week, reproduced, or commented on. "The chaos caused by ten troublous and confused years is being day by day dispelled," said the *Débats;* "and in order to remedy the defects in taste, which are the most lasting and difficult to eradicate, it is proposed to re-establish the old *Académie française.*" M. Michaud having returned from the exile to which the 18th Fructidor had condemned him, published his letters to Delille on *Pitié*, while preparing his poem on the *Printemps d'un Proscrit*, from which he caused quotations to be circulated in advance.

* I have a doubt about this: it had not been in the Lycée itself, which remained faithful to the spirit of the Revolution, that La Harpe professed his anti-philosophical recantations, or at least his last. I have heard contemporaries speak of some place in the Rue de Provence, near the Rue de Mont-Blanc.

On the occasion of the reprint in London of the *Poème des Jardins*, the *Virgile français* was persuaded to put an end to his already voluntary exile, and to look again as speedily as possible upon that France now worthy of him: Voltaire's example was quoted to him, he who was also in his time a refugee in London, but who had not wantonly prolonged a painful absence. The appearance of the *Génie du Christianisme*, a year before it was expected, added incomparable *éclat* to a restoration already very brilliant, and surrounded it with what is, after all, for us, at this distance of time, the sole glory which redeems it from oblivion.

Mme. de Staël, who was a child of the Revolution, who was inspired by philosophy, who spoke harshly of the reign of Louis XIV., and dreamt of an ideal republic, must have been considered then by all the men of this party, as an enemy, an adversary.

In the very first lines Fontanes displays an unfriendly, fastidious criticism. He extols the early work of Mme. de Staël, consecrated to the glorification of Rousseau: "Since that time Mme. de Staël's essays do not appear to have called forth the same amount of approbation." He first attacks the system of perfectibility; he indicates that Mme. de Staël is affected in her excited desire for the successive and continuous perfection of the human intellect, in the midst of her plaints about the sorrows of the heart and the corruption of the times, and points out, that in this she is something like the philosophers of whom Voltaire speaks:

"Who cried *All is well*, in a voice of misery."

He makes a great deal of this contradiction, which is but a seeming one. The partisans of perfectibility, as one can understand, are specially severe on the present, at their mildest they abuse it; unbelievers in perfectibility are less censorious of existing things, they accept them in a better spirit, endeavouring to accommodate themselves to circumstances. Fontanes, following up this piquant inconsistency, maintains that every time the dream of perfectibility takes possession of minds, empires are threatened with the most terrible scourges. "The learned Varron reckoned in his time two hundred and eighty-eight opinions upon the supreme good . . . from the time of Marius and Sylla; it is a compensation which the human mind allows itself." According to Fontanes, who quotes on this subject an expression of Condorcet's, it is to Voltaire, in the first place, that we owe the consoling idea of perfectibility. From this point the critic begins cleverly to reduce the question, till he gradually brings it to the dimensions of the following line from the *Mondain:*

"Oh, this happy time, this age of iron!"—

which, in his opinion, is the best and most elegant epitome that can possibly be made of all that has been uttered on this subject.

The grave, masculine spirit of Mme. de Staël found it specially hard to endure this scoffing, paltry, foolish style of harping back to a quotation from the *Mondain*. She boiled with impatience, and exclaimed among her intimates: "Oh! if I could make myself a man, even a very little one, I would settle matters once for all with these anti-philosophers!" The first article in the *Mercure* ends with this memorable *post scriptum*: "When this article was going to press, chance threw into our hands a still unpublished work, the title of which is *Some Moral and Poetic Beauties of the Christian Religion*. We give a few fragments from it, in which it will be seen that the author has discussed in a novel manner the same questions as Mme. de Staël." In

F

this way a kind of rivalry was at once established between Mme. de Staël and M. de Chateaubriand, who were first set at variance chiefly by their friends. Fontanes, the patron and upholder of M. de Chateaubriand, attacked the author of *La Littérature* in the *Décade;* Ginguené, who had taken it upon himself to praise *Delphine*, attacked the *Génie du Christianisme*, and boldly declared that that work, so immoderately praised in advance, had been eclipsed at its birth. But we shall resume at greater length the subject of the true relations between these two illustrious contemporaries.

In his second extract or article, Fontanes avenges the Greeks against the irruption of the *melancholy and sombre style,—a style peculiar to the spirit of Christianity, and which nevertheless is very favourable to the progress of modern philosophy.* It seems that, in the first edition, Mme. de Staël had used this expression, afterwards modified: "Anacreon is many centuries behind the philosophy which suits his style." "Ah!" exclaims Fontanes, "what woman worthy to inspire his muse ever expressed such sentiments regarding the poet-painter of love and pleasure?" As regards the dreamy sadness in the *impressions solitaires*, a kind of inspiration which Mme. de Staël denies the Greeks, he asks where it was ever better depicted than in the subject of *Philoctetes:* could he have already forgotten the confidential perusal he had just had of *René?* *

---

* The most venerable classical ancestor of the dreamy, melancholy recluses, is certainly Bellerophon. Homer first mentions them ; Ausonius, the latest of the ancient writers, says :

"Ceu dicitur olim
Mentis inops, cœtus hominum et vestigia vitans
Avia perlustrasse vagus loca Bellerophontes."

Bellerophon has a better claim than Philoctetes to be styled the René and the Oberman of the Greek fable.

These articles are, however, full of accurate and delicate details. When he upholds Homer against Ossian, he has little difficulty in triumphing; and in this quarrel of North *versus* South, he aptly remembers that the most melancholy poems were composed by the Arab Job more than three thousand years ago. Here he stops short, deferring, as he says, a more extended examination till a time when the most innocent questions will not be treated as affairs of State; but it appears that it was rather Mme. de Staël who had to complain that her philosophical doctrines were construed into factious opinions.

Fontanes' articles caused great excitement, and roused the passions of those whose opinions differed from his. Mme. Joseph Bonaparte abused them to Morfontaine the next time she saw him. But Bonaparte henceforth kept this clever writer in view as a convenient and moderate mouthpiece acquired for his future enterprises.

Is it necessary, after these articles of Fontanes', to mention two short articles of Geoffroy's, which only bring forward the same ideas, minus the worldly charm?*

In issuing a second edition of the book of *Littérature*, which appeared six months after the first, Mme. de Staël tried to refute Fontanes, and to clear the question of all the cavillings under which it had been obscured. Her only active revenge on the critic was to quote in a laudatory manner his poem, *Jour des morts dans une*

---

* These articles of Geoffroy's, dated December 1800, and inserted in I know not which newspaper or Collection (probably in his revived essay, *L'Année Littéraire*), were reproduced in vol. viii. of the *Spectateur française au dix neuvième siècle;* in the same Collection there are other articles relative to the polemics on perfectibility.

campagne; but she is pitilessly vehement against that false taste which may be represented as an exact and common style, serving to clothe ideas still more common. "Such a system," she says, "is much less exposed to criticism. The well-known phrases are like the intimate friends of a household; they are allowed to pass unquestioned. But no fluent or thoughtful writer exists whose style does not contain expressions astounding to those who read them for the first time, or at least to those who are not carried along by sympathy with the ardour of the noble thoughts expressed."

Mme. de Staël was not so easily satisfied as Boileau, writing to Brossette, "Bayle is a great genius. He is a man of a good stamp. His style is very plain and clear; one understands all he says.". She considered, and with justice, that there is a still better stamp, a distinction of style superior to that. Her second edition was the occasion of an article in the *Débats*, which concluded by saying, as if in reply to the preceding passage of the new preface: "All good writers agree that the form of our language was fixed and determined by the great writers of the last centuries. In an idiom it is necessary to distinguish what belongs to taste and imagination from that which has another origin. In our day there is nothing to prevent the invention of new words when they become absolutely necessary; but we ought not to invent new figures of speech, lest we should alter the nature of our language or offend against its genius." To this strange assertion there was a direct reply from the *Décade*, which seems to me to have been written by Ginguené; the philosophical critic is led to introduce a novelty in literature in order to refute the critic of the *Debats, whose mind does not desire perfection:* "If there had been journalists in the time of Corneille, had they used such language, and had Corneille and his successors been foolish enough to believe them, our literature would never have reached a higher standard of excellence than Malherbe, Requier, Voiture, and Brébeuf. The writer of that article is the man who wishes to continue *L'Année Littéraire* of Fréron ; he is worthy of it." We can, of course, see that it is to Geoffroy that Ginguené imputes, perhaps wrongly, the article in the *Débats*. He is naturally led to quote a remarkable note of Lemercier's, added to the Homeric poem which had just appeared. "Pedants," said that innovator of the time, "animadvert on words, and do not discern things. In writing they give themselves a great deal of trouble to produce what they call *negligence of style*. Subligny discovered four hundred errors in Racine's *Andromaque;* they immortalized the many verses in which he found them. Some criticisms (which were published) accused Boileau of not writing French ! Genius makes a language of its own. Who does not know that through Ennius and Lucretius, Horace and Virgil have been attacked ? Their Latin was unknown on the eve of the day on which their works appeared. People might say, as usual, that this remark opens the door to bad taste, if that door can ever be shut."

Do not these quotations give us an idea of how the men of the political and republican movement were led on by degrees to become organs of the literary progress, if the spontaneous development which began to be apparent had not, along with all their hopes, been crushed by the shocks of despotism which followed.

In the *Bibliothèque universelle et historique* of Le Clerc (1687), with regard to the *Remarques* of Vaugelas, we find (for such disputes have always occurred) a learned and judicious protest by an anonymous writer, against the rigorous regulations imposed on phraseology, and against those restrictions of metaphor on which the force of the law had been brought to bear. Intelligent literary people will read with agreeble surprise this fragment, as it is pleasant to find some presage of 1789 in Fénelon.

I confess that I am glad to be able to reply in words which are not my own, to what I consider the rather narrow-minded literary theories accepted by our bold politicians, and remodelled by some of our obstinate young critics. The defenders of an exclusive taste and a fixed language, are the *Tories* of literature; their cause is daily losing ground. Their business is to obstruct, to preserve; well, so be it! After each advance, when a talent forces itself into notice, they would silence it; they quickly raise up some obstacle which new talents will soon surmount. Thirty years ago, they (or their fathers) disclaimed Mme. de Staël and M. de Chateaubriand, and M. Lamartine fifteen years ago; now they support them, are engrossed by them, make them their defence against chance comers. This is an influence which may have its use and its value, for all talent requires to be tested, to be held in quarantine; but we must admit that the officer of this literary quarantine requires a much smaller share of intelligence and imagination to play his part, than would be necessary in contrary circumstances.

The most remarkable article which the book on *Littérature* produced, was a long letter from M. de Chateaubriand, inserted in the *Mercure de France*, Nivôse, year IX. The letter addressed to Citizen Fontanes is signed *The author of the Génie du Christianisme;* which book, although so long heralded, had not yet appeared. The young author, with perfect politeness and frequent compliments to the imagination of her against whom he contends, takes his stand as opposed to the system and the principles professed by her: "Mme. de Staël ascribes to philosophy what I attribute to religion. . . . You are not unaware that it is my whim to see Jesus Christ everywhere, as Mme. de Staël's is to see perfectibility. . . . I am sorry that Mme. de Staël has not, in a religious sense, unravelled for us the system of the passions; perfectibility was not, in my opinion, the instrument it was necessary to make use of in order to measure weaknesses." And again: "Sometimes Mme. de Staël seems a Christian; a moment later, and philosophy resumes its sway. Sometimes, inspired by her natural sensibility, she allows her soul to speak; but suddenly her argumentative faculties awake again, and thwart the impulse of the soul. . . . Consequently, this book is a singular mixture of truth and error." The eulogies bestowed on talent are here and there seasoned with a spice of *galant* spite: "On love, Mme. de Staël has written a Commentary on *Phèdre*. . . . Her observations are acute, and we see from the lesson of the scholiast that she understands her text." The letter ends with an eloquent double apostrophe: "Now this is what I would venture to say to her if I had the honour of her acquaintance: 'You are undoubtedly a superior woman. You have a wonderful head, and your imagination is sometimes full of charm, as, for instance, when you speak of Hermione disguised as a warrior. Your expressions are often noble and brilliant. . . . But despite all these advantages, your production is far from being as excellent as it might have been. The style is monotonous, unanimated, and too much interspersed with metaphysical remarks. The sophistry repels, the erudition does not satisfy, and the heart is made too subservient to the intellect.

... Your talent is but half developed; philosophy stifles it.' This is how I would speak to Mme. de Staël, with regard to glory. I would add ... 'You appear to be unhappy; in your works you make frequent complaints that you feel the need for hearts that understand you. This is because there are certain souls which search in vain in nature for the sister souls to which they were formed to be akin. ... And how can philosophy fill the void in our lives? Can the desert be filled with the desert, etc. etc.'"

Mme. de Staël, always accessible to, and eager for, admiration, desired to know the author of the letter in the *Mercure;* this first controversial exploit was thus the origin of a connection between the two geniuses whose names and fame we are accustomed to unite. Their connection was not, however, what we should of our own accord imagine; their camping grounds had always, for both of them, boundaries clearly defined and separate. Across these bounds their friends, less guarded than themselves, oftentimes pushed their way. Sneering at *Delphine* in the same bitter tone which Chénier afterwards employed against *Atala*, M. Michaud wrote: "You wished to make a duplicate of the *Génie du Christianisme*, and you have given us the *Beautés poétiques et morales de la Philosophie;* you have completely eclipsed that poor Chateaubriand, and I hope he will consider himself extinguished." A worshipper of Greek genius, of the beauties of Homer and Sophocles, the bard of Cymodocee and Eudore, and of the brilliant pomps of Catholicism, M. de Chateaubriand, already a finished artist, was not easily converted to admiration of Mme. de Staël's sometimes rather hazy heroes and rather vague outlines, the predominance of mind and purpose over form, that great multitude of clever ideas discussed conversationally; so he admired Mme. de Staël less than she admired him. On the other hand, whether by chance forgetfulness, or from some embarrassment on the subject, she rarely expresses any opinion of him in her numerous writings. When, in the evenings at Coppet, they read and compared *Paul and Virginia* and the episode of Velleda, Mme. de Staël rapturously placed the fierce and powerful beauty of the priestess far above the, in her opinion, too countrified sweetness of the other masterpiece; the celebrated article which caused the suppression of the *Mercure* in 1807, also drew from her exclamations of admiration,* but in her works there is scarcely any trace of such an admiring testimony. In the preface to *Delphine*, the *Génie du Christianisme* is referred to as a work *the originality and extraordinary brilliancy of which, even its enemies must admire.*

M. de Chateaubriand, in an article in the *Mercure* on M. de Bonald (December 1802), returns the compliment by a few lines of eulogy of Mme. de Staël; but through all this mutual homage they always maintained the same position, an antagonistic one.† Can we not still imagine to ourselves, these two great names, like two summits on opposite shores, two threatening heights, under which hostile groups attack and fight, but which from afar, from our point of view as posterity, seem to unite, almost to join together, and become the double triumphal column at the entrance of the century? We, the generation

* The Souvenirs of M. Meneval (vol. i. page 29) show her to us the eager patroness and admiring reader of *Atala* and *René*, in the society of Joseph Bonaparte at Morfontaine (1801-1802).

† M. de Chateaubriand is, however, mentioned honourably, but with neither blame nor praise, in two places in the book on *Germany*, Part II. chap. i., and Part IV. chap. iv.

which has sprung up since the *Martyrs* and since *Corinne*, bow before these two inseparable geniuses, and are influenced by the filial sentiment of which M. de Lamartine has made himself the generous interpreter in his *Déstinées de la Poésie*.

If, as regards depth and artistic style, there are great and important differences between M. de Chateaubriand and Mme. de Staël, we are yet struck by the many essential resemblances they present: both loving liberty, impatient of the same tyranny, capable of feeling the incalculable greatness of popular destinies without abjuring aristocratic traditions and inclinations; both working for the revival of religious sentiment, in ways which are rather different than contrary. The Restoration brought them together again. Mme. de Duras was a kind of bond,* and it was to M. de Chateaubriand that in her last illness Mme. de Staël was able to say those beautiful words: "I have always been the same, ardent and sad; I have loved God, my father, and liberty." However, in politics they were then opponents, just as, in former times, philosophy had separated them. In her *Considérations sur la Révolution française*, which was published shortly after the death of its author, M. de Chateaubriand is not mentioned; and in an article of his in the *Conservateur* (December 1819), we again find one of those compliments to Mme. de Staël, always

---

* Mme. de Staël had a singular liking for Mme. de Duras, whom she found, as she was herself, *a true person in an artificial society*. I have read a touching note which she addressed to her on the 26th of June 1817, that is to say, eighteen days before her death, and which she had dictated to her son (Auguste de Staël), being by that time too weak to write. She had added below, in her own hand, in large, uneven, shaky writing: *Bien des compliments de ma part à René*.

respectful and seemly, but in which admiration is
tempered by reserve,—the homage, in short, of a
courteous and finished adversary.

This too-prolonged discord has ceased ; a woman *
who, by a singular chance, had met M. de Chateaubriand for the first time at Mme. de Staël's house in
1801, who had seen him again for the second time at
the same place in 1814, became the bond of sympathy
between both. In his honourable affection for the
intimate friend of that high-souled genius, for the
confidante of so many loving thoughts, M. de Chateaubriand modified his judgments, and exalted his opinions
on a character and talent better known to him when
all formerly existing barriers had broken down. The
preface to the *Etudes Historiques* gives proof of this
wider communion ; but more especially his last me-
morial will comprise a portrait of Mme. de Staël, and
a judgment, which will remain the noblest, as it is
certainly the highest and the most worthy of her.
This is, at all events, with so much that is sad, in
surviving his illustrious contemporaries, one advantage
for a man who is himself celebrated, if he possesses the
true reverence for glory ; it enables him at leisure to
crown their image, restore their statue, and reveren-
tially to solemnize their tomb. M. de Chateaubriand's
touching eulogies on Mme. de Staël, his pilgrimage
to Coppet in 1831, with the sympathetic friend who
forms the sacred bond between the two, with her
whom nevertheless he did not accompany to the depths
of that mournful sanctuary, and who, with the modest
shyness of grief, desired to penetrate alone to that
grave among the cypress trees,—this, by the banks of
that Lake of Geneva, so near the places celebrated by
the author of *Julie*, will form in the eyes of posterity

* Mme. Récamier.

a mournfully pathetic commemoration rite. Carefully remember, for they honour our century, these devout affinities of rival geniuses, Goethe and Schiller, Scott and Byron, Chateaubriand and Mme. de Staël. Voltaire insulted Jean-Jàcques, and it was the voice of human nature alone (to speak like Chénier) which reconciled them. Racine and Molière, who did not love each other, were silent about each other, and we feel pleased to know of this social politeness. There is indeed much poetic greatness in the world.

II.

At the period when the book *De la Littérature* was published, Mme. de Staël's intellectual cravings inspired her with a noble public ambition, which she followed more or less earnestly till about 1811, at which time a great and serious change took place in her. In the former more exclusively sentimental disposition from which we have considered her, Mme. de Staël had scarcely thought of literature except as the organ of sensibility, the mouthpiece of sorrow. She desponds; she complains of false accusations; she passes from ill-sustained stoicism to eloquent lamentation; she wished to love; she thought to die. But she then became conscious that although one suffers very much, one does not die; that the faculties of thought, the power of the soul, increase in grief; that she would never be loved as she herself loved; and that, therefore, she must find for herself some great employment for her life. She then thought seriously of making a full use of her talents, of not allowing herself to be discouraged; and since there was yet time, for the sun had scarcely begun to go down, her spirit resolved to walk proudly in the years of middle life. "Let us at last arise," she cries in the preface to the book so often quoted,—"let us arise under the burden of existence; let us not give to our unjust enemies, nor to our ungrateful friends, the triumph of having crushed our intellectual faculties. They compel those to seek glory who would have been contented with affection; ah, well! we must attain it!" From henceforth glory and sentiment openly and equally shared the longings of her soul. Society had always been much to her; Europe henceforth became something, and this was the great theatre in sight of which she aspired after vast enterprises. Her beautiful ship, beaten by the tempest outside the harbour, weary with long waiting in sight of the shore, exasperated by the delay and the wreck signals, departed full sail for the high seas.

Delphine, Corinne, the book *De L'Allemagne,* were the successive conquests of this most glorious adventure. In 1800, Mme. de Staël was still young, but that youthfulness of over thirty years was neither an illusion nor a future for her; she therefore substituted, while it was yet time, the boundless horizon of glory for that of the youth which was already fading, the limits of which she could perceive, but which was thus perpetuated and prolonged; and thus, in the enjoyment of all her powerful talent, she advanced during these, the most brilliant but unvalued years.

Corinne, and the time immediately after its appearance, mark the dominant point in the life of Mme. de Staël. Every human life, possessed of even a little greatness, has its sacred hill; every existence which has shone or reigned has its Capitol. The Capitol, the Cape Misenum of *Corinne,* is also that of Mme. de Staël. From this time, the lingering youth which fled, the increasing persecution, the broken or changing friendships, even sickness itself, all contributed, as we shall see, to mature still more her talent, to introduce this genius, majestic and crowned with fame, into the sombre years. Dating from 1811 especially, and searching deeply into Mme. de Staël's thoughts, we shall gradually discover the calm which religion brings, the sorrow that matures, the strength which restrains itself, and that heart, till then stormy as an ocean, submissive also like it, and returning with meritorious reluctance to its determined limits. We shall see at last, at the end of this triumphal path as at the end of the most humbly pious, we shall see a cross. But as we leave the dreams of sentiment, of hope, and romantic deception, we only reach the years of full activity and of triumph.

If the book *De la Littérature* produced such a great effect, the romance *Delphine*, published in the end of 1802, did not cause less excitement. We may imagine how fascinating this book was to a society excited by political vicissitudes and all the conflicts of life, when the *Génie du Christianisme* had just restored religious discussions to honour, about the same period as the Concordat and the modification of the divorce laws! Benjamin Constant has written, that it is perhaps in the pages she has dedicated to her father, that Mme. de Staël reveals herself most to us: but we always have this feeling with every book of hers we read; the last volume we open is the one in which we think we recognise her best. This does appear to me specially true in regard to *Delphine*. "*Corinne*," says Mme. Necker de Saussure, "is the ideal of Mme. de Staël; *Delphine* is the real counterpart of her youth." *Delphine* became to Mme. de Staël a pathetic personification of the years of her pure sentiment and tenderness, at a time when she was weaning herself from them,—a last distracting, backward glance of farewell at the commencement of her public reign, on the threshold of

European glory, like the statue of a heart-broken Ariadne in the court of a temple of Theseus.

In *Delphine*, the author intended to produce a perfectly natural romance, full of analysis, of moral observation, and passion. To me, delightful as I find nearly every page, it is still not as natural, as *real* a romance, as I expected to find it from Mme de Staël's own prognostics in the *Essai sur les Fictions*. It has some of the defects of *La Nouvelle Héloïse*, and the letter form introduces too much conventionality in the literary arrangements. One of the inconveniences of novels in the form of letters is, that at once the characters have to assume a tone in accord with the part they are to play. From Mathilde's first letter, her hard blunt nature has to be portrayed, and we see her quite inflexible even in her devotion. And that no misunderstanding may arise, Delphine, in replying, speaks to her of that rigid rule, perhaps necessary to a *less sweet nature;* things which are neither said nor written just at once between persons accustomed to the ways of the world, like *Delphine* and *Mathilde*. Léonce begins in his very first letter to M. Barton, to enlarge very fully about his prepossession for honour, which is his characteristic. In real life such traits are shown only proportionately, and brought out by degrees through facts. The other method stamps the most bewitching romance with a tone of conventionality, and gives it a peculiar style; thus, in *La Nouvelle Heloïse*, all the letters written by Claire d'Orbe are necessarily gay and playful; from the first line a tone of frolicsomeness is the correct thing. In one word, the characters of romances in the form of letters, from the moment they take up the pen, are always considering how they can present themselves to the reader in the most expressive attitudes, under the most significant aspects: this forms a rather unnatural classical style of grouping, unless the plot is worked out very slowly and with much profusion of language, as in *Clarisse*. Add to this the necessity (which is a very unlikely one, and unfavourable for emotional feeling), that those personages have to shut themselves up to write, at moments when they have neither the leisure nor the strength for such employment, when they are in bed, or recovering from a fainting fit, etc. etc. But after we have once admitted this defect in regard to *Delphine*, what delicacy and what passion are mingled! what frank sensibility, and subtle penetration of character ! With regard to these characters, it was difficult in the world of that time to prevent people finding portraits in them. I have little belief in perfect portraits from novelists of fertile imagination; the copy does not go beyond the first more or less numerous characteristics, which are soon transformed and finished off differently; only the author who creates the characters could distinguish the invisible and tortuous line which separates recollection from invention. But at that period people insisted on discovering some existing model for each figure. If in *Delphine* there was an obvious resemblance to Mme. de Staël, who were portrayed by, not perhaps the ideal Léonce, but at least M. de Lebensei, Mme. de Cerlèbe, Mathilde, and Mme. de Vernon? It has been said that Mme. de Cerlèbe, devoted to domestic pursuits and the placid uniformity of duty, and experiencing infinite delight in the educating of her children, was very much like Mme. Necker de Saussure, who besides, like Mme. de Cerlèbe, also worshipped her father. People have thought they recognised in M. de Lebensei, the Protestant gentleman with the manners of an Englishman, the man who was *the most remarkably talented man it was possible to meet,* a most remarkable likeness to Benjamin Constant; but in this case, only one part of the portrait, the brilliant side, would have been true; and at least half of the solid virtues with which M. de Lebensei is credited could not apply to the presumed original, excepting by way of counsel, or as expressing regret over their absence.* As regards Mme. de Vernon, the best drawn character in the book, according to Chénier and all the critics, people imagined they discovered there a portrait, changed and disguised as a woman, of our most famous politician, of him whom Mme. de Staël had first caused to be struck off the list of political *émigrés* whom she had pushed forward into power before the 18th Fructidor, and who had rewarded her for that active warmth of friendship only by the most carefully polite selfishness.†

When *Delphine* was composed, the incident of the dinner which is mentioned in the *Dix Années de Exil* had already taken place. "The day," says Mme. de Staël, "on which the signal of the opposition was given in the Tribunate, by one of my friends, I had invited to my house several persons whose society pleased me much, but who had all joined the new Government. I received ten notes of excuse at five o'clock; I was not put about by the first or the second, but as the notes succeeded each other, I began to be anxious."

The man she had so generously served, avoided her, then, in that perfectly polite way in which one sends an excuse for not accepting a dinner invitation. Admitted to new greatness, he would in no way commit himself to support her who was so soon to be exiled. He does, perhaps, justify her in *Héros*, but in that same doubt-

* This other aspect of the character of M. de Lebensei really resembles M. de Jaucourt.
† Talleyrand.—Tr.

ful manner which succeeded so well when Mme. Vernon justifies Delphine to Léonce. Mme. de Staël, like Delphine, could not live without forgiving: she wrote from Vienna in 1808 to this same personage as to an old friend on whom one can rely;* she recalls the past to him without any bitterness. "You wrote to me thirteen years ago from America, *If I remain here a year longer, I shall die;* I can say the same of my absence abroad, I am overcome with grief here." She added these words, so full of indulgent sadness: "Adieu, —are you happy? With talents so superior, do you not sometimes sound the depth of everything, that is to say, even sorrow?".

But without venturing to contend that Mme. de Vernon may be in all ways a slenderly disguised portrait, without having too strong a desire to identify with the model in question that clever woman, whose seductive amiability makes one feel by comparison harsh and discontented, that woman whose acts are so complicated and her conversation so simple, whose speech is so soft and her silence so dreamy, whose talent is only for conversation, neither for reading nor thinking, and who escapes from *ennui* by gambling, etc. etc.,— without going so far as this, it has been impossible to help being at least influenced by the application of a more innocent feature. "No one knows better than myself," says Mme. de Vernon in one place (Letter xxviii. Part I.), "how to make use of indolence; it helps me naturally to baffle the activity of others. . . . I have not four times in my life given myself the trouble of insisting, but when I have gone so far as to take this fatigue, nothing turns me from my aim, I attain it; take my word for it." In this passage I saw myself a trait applicable to the clever indolence of the personage

* See *Revue Retrospective*, No. 9, June 1834.

so much extolled, when, one evening, I heard a clever diplomatist, of whom some one asked if he intended soon to appear at his post, reply, that he was in no hurry, he was waiting. "I was still quite young," he added, "when M. de Talleyrand instructed me in one essential line of conduct: Do not be zealous!" Is not this exactly Mme. de Vernon's principle?

Since we are on the subject of the possibly real traits of character portrayed in *Delphine*, do not let us overlook, among others, one which (artlessly) reveals to us the devoted heart of Mme. de Staël. In the chief catastrophe of *Delphine* (I speak of the older event, which remains the unique and beautiful one), the heroine, after having exhausted every supplication to the judge of Léonce, perceives that the child of the magistrate is ill, and she exclaims, with a sublime cry, "Very well! your child,—if you deliver up Léonce to the tribunal,—your child, I say, will die! he will die!" This cry of Delphine's was really uttered by Mme. de Staël, when, at the end of the 18th Fructidor, she rushed up to General Lemoine to plead with him for the pardon of a young man she knew to be in danger of being shot, and who was no other than M. de Norbins. The sentiment of compassion impetuously governed her, and, once roused, left her no peace. In 1802, uneasy about Chénier menaced with proscription, she hurried at daybreak to offer him shelter, money, and a passport.* How often in 1792, and at all times, do we not see her thus! "My political opinions are proper names," she said. Not!... that her political opinions were strong principles; but proper names, that is to say, persons, friends, the unknown, all who lived and suffered, were considered in her generous imagination

* See notice on M. J. Chénier, heading his works, by M. Daunou.

and she did not know what an abstract principle of justice meant, with one who silenced his human sympathies.

When *Delphine* appeared, criticism was boundless, for it had found a fruitful subject. Indeed, all the opinions on religion, on politics, or on marriage, although dating in the romance from 1790 and 1792, were singularly appropriate in 1802, depicting as they did old passions and new problems. The *Journal des Debats* (December 1802) published an article, signed "A," said to have been written by M. de Feletz, a bantering kind of article, full of stinging, waspish remarks, but at the same time strictly polite; the critic of the salon became also the reproachful mouthpiece of reviving society circles. "Nothing could be more dangerous or more immoral than the principles set forth in this book. . . . Forgetting the principles in which she has been brought up in a Protestant family, and as the daughter of M. Necker, the author of *Religious Opinions* profanes revelation; the daughter of Mme. Necker, who is the writer of a book against divorce, makes long arguments in favour of divorce." Altogether, *Delphine* was styled "a very bad book, written with cleverness and talent." This article appears to have been insufficient, for the same paper inserts, a few days later (4th and 9th of January 1803), two letters addressed to Mme. de Staël, and signed *L'Admireur*; they were from the pen of M. Michaud. The man of talent and taste who was induced to make these attacks was young, and carried away by party feeling thus to revenge himself for political defeat, but, having gracefully withdrawn his accusations, he will excuse us for noticing his too hurtful vehemence. The first letter confined itself to a discussion of the characters of the romance judged to be immoral. *Delphine* is compared with the heroine of an unwholesome romance, in the same way as in our own day *Lelia* has been styled pernicious. The second letter attacks the style more particularly; the fault-finding is at times legitimate, and of a free and easy, rather pleasant kind. "*What a powerful sentiment love is! What else is worth living for!* When your characters make melancholy reflections on the past, one exclaims, *I have spoiled my life;* another says, *I have missed my object in life;* while a third, trying to outdo the two first, says, *I believe that I alone have properly understood life.*"* The *high principles*, the *imagery based on thoughts of eternity*, the *strata of the centuries*, the *limits of the soul*, the *mysteries of fate*, the *souls exiled from love*,—this kind of phraseology, half sentimental, half spiritualistic, and certainly allowable, partly Genevese, incoherent, and very contestable, is in this article lengthily scoffed at. M. de Feletz had himself abstracted a few inaccuracies of style, such words as *insistence, persistence, vulgarity,* which, notwithstanding his condemnation, have passed uncensured. If we were to criticise the detail of *Delphine*, we could pick out many repetitions, many incongruities, a thousand oft-recurring little faults, from which Mme. de Staël was not exempt, and into which an artistic author never falls.

Mme. de Stael, on whom the malice of the remarks made had no effect, afterwards graciously pardoned the

* The impartial or inquiring critic will be able to read a justification of Mme. de Staël on this point, and also a very high appreciation of *Delphine* in general, in the book I have already quoted, *Notice et Souvenirs Biographiques du Comte Van Der Duyn* (1852). At page 386 of the *Journal de Lecture* by this estimable Dutchman, there is an article full of sound judgment, entitled *De certaines Hardiesses de Style reprochées à Mme. de Staël.*

writer of these letters when she met him at M. Suard's, in that neutral and conciliating salon of an intellectual man, whom age and experience, and the learning acquired from famous contemporaries, had sufficed to render great in his turn. The journal which M. Suard then edited, *Le Publiciste*, although from a literary point of view it might have made captious remarks on several points in *Delphine*, did not take part in the dispute, and spoke very favourably of it in an article inspired by the good feeling of M. Hochet.

About the same time, *Le Mercure* published an article signed "F,"* but so bitter and personal that the *Journal de Paris*, which, through the pen of M. de Villetergue, had judged the romance severely enough, especially its morality, was unable to help expressing its astonishment, that an article written in such a style should be found in the *Mercure* side by side with an article signed La Harpe, and under the initial letter of a man dear to the friends of good sense and decorum. The words were these (and I do not choose the worst to quote): "*Delphine* speaks of Love in the manner of a Bacchante, of God in that of a Quaker, of Death in that of a grenadier, and of morality as a sophist." Fontanes, who was suspected on account of the initial, wrote to the *Journal de Paris* to repudiate the article, which was in reality written by the author of *Dot et Suzette*, and *Frederic*. Have we not in our own day witnessed an outburst of a similar description, against a woman,† one of the most eminent the literary world has beheld since the authoress of *Delphine*? In the *Débats* of the 12th February 1803, Gaston gives a sketch of a pamphlet of 800 pages (was this only a joke of the journalist?), entitled (*The Converted*) *Delphine;* he gave extracts from it: one of the characters is supposed to say to Mme. de

* Fiévée. † Georges Sand.

Staël, "I have just entered on the career which many women have pursued successfully, but I have taken as my model neither the *Princess de Clèves*, nor *Caroline*, nor *Adèle de Sénange*." This malicious pamphlet, if indeed it ever existed, in which envy swells into a large book, appears only to be a collection of incongruous phrases pirated from Mme. de Staël, and strung together in the most unnatural style. Mme. de Genlis, returning from Altona to preach morality, wrote for the *Bibliothèque des Romans*, a lengthy novel, in which, by the aid of truncated explanations and artificial interpretations, she manages to represent Mme. de Staël as defending suicide. Mme. de Staël revenged herself by praising warmly *Mademoiselle de Clermont*. "She attacks me," she remarked, "and I defend her; thus our intercourse ceases." Mme. de Genlis, after this, in her *Mémoires*, accused Mme. de Staël of *ignorance*, as before she had called her *immoral*. But we pardon her, for she made amends in the end, in a kindly novel entitled *Athénais*, of which we shall have occasion to speak again. A friendly influence, accustomed to work such gentle miracles, had appealed to her.*

In speaking of a work so pathetic as *Delphine*, we ask to be excused that we have not chosen to confine ourselves to the touching scenes of Bellerive or the Gardens of the Champs-Elysées, rather than recall these bitter clamours, and raise up so much old dust; but it is a good plan, when we wish to follow or retrace a triumphal march, to endure the crowd as well, to show the car just as it was, encompassed with difficulties, and also applauded.

The violence of the attacks drew out justification; Mme. de Staël's friends were indignant, and she was most energetically defended. Of two articles inserted

* Mme. Récamier.

in the *Décade*, the first begins as follows: "No work for a long time has so engrossed public attention as this romance; it is a kind of success which it is not a matter of indifference to obtain, for it is one which has to be paid for. Several journalists, whose opinion of a book we can guess from the name of the author, have inveighed against *Delphine*, or rather, against Mme. de Staël, like people reckless of their words.... They have attacked a woman, one with the rudeness of a Collegiate (Ginguené seems to have imputed to Geoffroy, against whom he had a spite, one of the hostile articles we have mentioned above), another with the persiflage of common wit, and all with the boasting security of cowardice." After numerous appreciative quotations, coming to the part in which there are certain strained modes of expression, certain new words or terms, Ginguené judiciously remarks: "These are not really errors of the language, but blunders which a woman of so much wit and true talent will have no difficulty in overcoming if she wishes to do so." What Ginguené did not remark on, and what he might well have opposed to the vulgar accusations of impiety and immorality which the coarse or priggish critics talked so loudly about, is the exalted eloquence of the religious thoughts which we find expressed in many pages of *Delphine*, as if in emulation of the Catholic theories of the *Génie du Christianisme:* for instance, the letter of Delphine to Léonce (xiv. Part III.), where she tries to persuade him to a belief in natural religion and the universal hope of immortality; and again, when M. de Lebensei (xvii. Part IV.), writing to Delphine, combats the Christian idea of sorrow perfecting the religious life, and invokes the law of nature, as leading men to goodness by gently alluring the inclinations. Delphine is not convinced; she does not believe that the attractive system put before her responds to all the real combinations of fate, and that happiness and virtue go hand in hand on this earth. Unquestionably it is not the Catholicism of Thérèse d'Ervins which triumphs in Delphine; the design here is Protestant, a Unitarian Protestantism, differing very little from that of the Savoyard Vicaire; but among the Pharisees who exclaim of its impiety, I have difficulty in discovering any among them for whom even these philosophic and natural beliefs, if seriously adopted, would not have been, as compared to their own faith, an immense moral and religious gain. As for the accusation that Delphine attacks the sanctity of marriage, it has seemed to me, on the contrary, that the most conspicuous idea in the book is the desire for happiness in the married state, and a profound conviction of the impossibility of obtaining happiness otherwise. I also remark her recognition or acknowledgment that the most frequent cause of the wreck of this happiness, even with the most tender and virtuous love, is the want of social harmony in life. This idea of *happiness in the married state* has always haunted Mme. de Staël, as romantic fancies importunately haunt the minds of those who have no actual experience of romance. In the *Influence of the Passions*, she speaks with great pathos of an old married couple who were still lovers, whom she had met in England. In the book on *Littérature*, we mark the pleasure with which she quotes the beautiful verses which terminate Thomson's song on *Spring*, where that perfect union, which in her case is conspicuous by absence, is glorified. In one of the chapters of *Germany* she returns to this subject with such a virtuous, almost grateful, tone in her reflections, that we are touched, especially when we compare that page with the hidden facts which inspired it. In *Delphine*, the happy picture of the Belmont family is neither more nor less than that domestic Eden always longed for by her among all her trials.

M. Necker in his *Cours de Morale religieuse*, loves also to dwell on the subject of happiness secured by the sanctity of the marriage bond. Mme. de Staël, in so frequently returning to this *dream*, had not far to seek for her imagery; setting aside her own experiences, her imagination found its model close at hand; failing her own, she could recall to her memory her mother's felicity, and plan and prophesy her daughter's.*

But, after all, with all our partiality, we must acknowledge that *Delphine* is a disturbing study, and one which we do not counsel perfect innocence to test, although for minds to whom real trouble has come, and who are like to be overwhelmed by prosaic disenchantment, it may often effect a healthy awakening from sentimental brooding. It is a fortunate disturbance which tempts us back to the emotions of love, and restores to us the faculty of youthful devotion!

In return for the gracious manner in which the *Décade* had spoken, and for the support given to her by the writers, *littérateurs*, and philosophers of that school, Mme. de Staël has always spoken well of them in her works. Excepting Chénier, about whom she makes a few rather severe remarks in her *Considérations*, she has never mentioned one of this literary and philosophic group but with generous recognition of old ties of friendliness and kindly feeling. But her exile in the end of the year 1803, her travels, her existence as the lady paramount at Coppet, her connections in Germany, and her aristocratic relations, from this time brought her into another sphere, which soon dispelled that

---

* Mme. la Duchesse de Broglie was very early enraptured with ideas of family felicity, and always retained an instinctive respect for those who had once experienced it.

suggestion inspired by the events of the year III., of which we have tried to catch a glimpse. Forced to leave Paris, she at once directed her steps towards Germany, practised reading and speaking German, visited Weimar and Berlin, and made the acquaintance of Goethe and the Prussian princes. She collected the first materials for the work, which a second visit, in 1807-8, enabled her to complete. To launch forth thus suddenly beyond the Rhine was her brusque way of breaking with Napoleon, who was greatly irritated. It was breaking also with the philosophical customs of the eighteenth century, which, to all appearance, she had just so gloriously espoused. Thus do great minds act; they are already at another pole when we suppose them to be still at the opposite one. Like the rapid strategy of indefatigable generals, they kindle their fires on the heights, and are supposed to be encamped behind them, when they are already many miles on their march, and will attack the enemy's flank.

The death of her father brought Mme. de Staël back very suddenly to Coppet. When her first mourning had calmed down, and after the publication of some of M. Necker's manuscripts, she left again (1804), to visit Italy. A love of nature and of art awoke in her under new skies.[*] Delphine confesses somewhere that she does not care for pictures, and when she walks in the gardens she is much more interested in the urns and

[*] Mme. de Staël's love of art was always an acquired taste, exotic, like a plant which never grew in the open air. Her nature is very well described in a letter which Goethe wrote from Weimar, on the 27th of February 1804, to his friend, Zelter the composer, who lived in Berlin. "Professor Wolf and Counsellor Müller have stayed a fortnight at Weimar; Woss spent several days; and we have already had Mme. de Staël four weeks. This extraordinary woman is going to Berlin soon, and I shall give her a note of introduction to you. Go and see her

monuments than in nature pure and simple. But that autumnal haze which envelopes the horizon of Bellerive fades under the purity of Roman skies ; all the gifts of the muses which are to adorn the train of *Corinne* now hasten to develop.*

Having returned to Coppet in 1805, and being occupied with the writing of her Roman romance, Mme. de Staël could no longer remain at such a distance from Paris, that unique central point, where she had shone, and in the sight of which she aspired to greater glory. It was at this time she displayed that increasing restlessness, that *mal de la capitale*,—home sickness, so to speak,—which no doubt detracts a little from the dignity of her exile, but which at the same time betrays the passionate sincerity of all her impulses. An order from the police compelled her to remain forty miles from Paris. Instinctively and stubbornly, like the noble steed attached to a stake, who strains his tether in every direction, or like the maligned fly, which incessantly dashes itself against the window-pane, she reaches the settled limit, she goes to Auxerre, to Chelons, to Blois, to Saumur ; and within the boundaries which she is for ever disputing and encroaching upon, her unexpected visits to her friends become a knowing strategy, a game of chess, which she played with Bonaparte and Fouché, or their representatives, more or less rigorous. When she was allowed to settle at Rouen, we see her at first triumphant, for she has gained a few miles in the geometrical radius. But such provincial towns offered

soon ; she is easy to get on with, and your music will certainly give her great pleasure, although literature, poetry, philosophy, and things akin, interest her more than art.".

* It must have been during her stay at Rome (in 1805) that M. Aug. Wil. Schlegel, who accompanied Mme. de Staël, addressed to her the Elegy entitled *Rome*.

little by way of resource to a mind so active and so envious for the accent and the words of the pure Athènes.* Contempt for every description of meanness or of mediocrity was distasteful to her, choked her. She was able to confirm and make her own comments on the amusing play of Picard. Even Benjamin Constant's wonderful conversational powers were scarcely able to charm away her vapours. "Poor Schlegel," she said, "is half dead of *ennui*; Benjamin Constant comes off better with his animals." Travelling at a later date (1808) in Germany: "All I see here is better, more learned, more enlightened, perhaps, than France; but the smallest inch of France is worth more to me." Two years afterward, in provincial France, she did not hold to that; or did she mean it only of Paris, which was the only place in the world for her?

At last, thanks to the toleration of Fouché, who acted on the principle of doing the least possible amount of evil when it was useless, a way was found to allow her to settle eighteen miles from Paris (what a conquest!) at Acosta, an estate belonging to Mme. de Castellane; from there she superintended the publishing of *Corinne*. In returning her proof-sheets, she must often have echoed Ovid: "Go, my book, happy book, which goest to town without me!" "Oh, the gutter of the Rue du Bac!" † she would exclaim, when the mirror of Leman was pointed out to her. And at Acosta as at Coppet, so she felt; more longingly than ever, she stretched her arms towards that bourn so near to her.‡

The year 1806 seems to have been too long for her

* Parisian.
† Before her exile, Mme. de Staël lived in the Rue Grenelle-Saint-Germain, near the Rue du Bac.
‡ A liking for the country was never an essential part of Mme. de Staël's nature, and her obstinate yearning for the Rue du

imagination to endure such a punishment, and she arrived in Paris one evening, only allowing a few of her friends to know. She walked out every evening and part of the night by moonlight, not daring to venture out by day. But during this adventurous incursion, she was seized by a violent desire, very characteristic of her, to see a great lady who was an old friend of her father's, Countess Tessé, the same who said of her, "If I were a queen, I would command Mme. de Staël to talk to me all day long." She was very old, however, at this time, and terrified at the idea of being compromised by Mme. de Staël's visit; the result of the escapade was a series of indiscretions which at last reached Fouché's ears. It was necessary, therefore, to depart in all haste, to risk no more of these moonlight walks along the quays, by the favoured stream, and round that Place Louis XV., so familiar to Delphine.

Soon after this came the publication of *Corinne*, to confirm and increase the rigour of Mme. de Staël's first exile.* We find her next taking refuge at Coppet, Bac quite spoiled her pleasure in it. Walking out one day at Acosta with the two Schlegels and M. Fauriel, the latter, whose arm she had taken, began unconsciously to admire a view. "Ah, my dear Fauriel," she said, "I see you are still prejudiced in favour of the country." Then, seeing at once that she had said something unusual, she smiled by way of qualifying her remark. A long time after this, after the Empire, conversing one day with M. Molé, and expressing her surprise that a man of so much talent should care for the country, she ingenuously remarked to him, "Were it not for the sake of appearances, I would not open my window to see the Bay of Naples for the first time, while I would go five hundred miles to speak to a learned man I don't even know." An unaffected and at the same time flattering way of expressing how much she preferred conversation and society to nature.

* The proofs of the severity with which she was treated are

where, after all, she appears to us in her true dignity, the centre of her stately court.

What the sojourn at Ferney was for Voltaire, the life at Coppet was for Mme. de Staël, but with a more romantic halo round her, it seems to us, more of the grandeur and pomp of life. Both reigned in their exile; Voltaire, in his low flat plain, his secluded, poverty-stricken castle, with a view of despoiled, unshaded gardens, scorned and derided. The influence of Coppet is quite different; it is that of Jean-Jacques continued, ennobled, installed, and reigning amid the same associations as his rival. Coppet counterbalances Ferney, half dethrones it. We also, of this younger generation, judge Ferney by comparing it with Coppet, coming down from Coppet. The beauty of its site, the woods which shadow it, the sex of its poet, the air of enthusiasm we breathe there, the elegant company, the glorious names, the walks by the lake, the mornings in the park, the mysteries and the inevitable storms which we surmise, all contribute to well known and indisputable. We read in the published Correspondence of Napoleon, at the beginning of a letter from the Emperor to Cambacérès, dated from Osterode, 26th March 1807: "I have written to the Minister of Police to send Mme. de Staël back to Geneva, with permission to go to any foreign country she chooses. That woman still pursues her profession of *intrigante*. She went to Paris against my orders,—she is a perfect pest. My desire is that you speak seriously to the Minister about this, for I see I shall be forced to have her apprehended. Keep an eye on Benjamin Constant also, and at the least (political) interference on his part, I shall send him to Brunswick, to his wife (!). I shall tolerate nothing from that clique. I do not wish them to make converts, and bring down my wrath on good citizens." Napoleon affects to consider Mme. de Staël as practically a foreigner, just as at the same time he pretended to see only a foreigner in Benjamin Constant: this was put right during the Hundred Days.

idealize the place for us. Coppet is the Elysium which every disciple of Jean-Jacques would gladly give to the mistress of his dreams. Mme. de Genlis, awakening from her early errors, and wishing to repair them, has tried in a novel, called *Athenais, ou le Château de Coppet en 1807*,* to reproduce the habits and some of the delicate complications of that life which from afar we can only distinguish through an enchanted glass. But we must not expect to find a faithful picture in that otherwise pleasant production: the dates are confused, the characters are grouped with an object, and their parts are arranged to fit in; M. Schlegel is made to seem grotesque, sacrificed without scruple and regardless of good taste; the whole situation, indeed, is represented under a false romantic light, which in our eyes spoils true romance as much as it would spoil reality. For my part, I would much rather have some exact details, on which the after fancy of those who have not seen, might indulge in pleasant dreams of what might have been.

The life at Coppet was the life of a country mansion. There were often as many as thirty guests there, friends and strangers; the most constant visitors were Benjamin Constant, M. Auguste Wilhelm de Schlegel, M. de Sabran, M. de Sismondi, M. de Bonstetten, the Barons de Voght, de Balk, etc.; also once, or perhaps several times a year, M. Mathieu de Montmorency, M. Prosper de Barante, Prince Auguste of Prussia, the celebrated beauty of the day, designated by Mme. de Genlis under the name of *Athenais*, and a crowd of fashionable people, acquaintances from Germany or Geneva. The literary and philosophical conversations, always high-toned, clever and witty, began as early as eleven in the morning, when all met at breakfast; and

* Published by Jules Didot, 1832.

were carried on again at dinner, and in the interval between dinner and supper, which was at eleven at night, and often as late as midnight. Benjamin Constant and Mme. de Staël engrossed the conversation. It was then that Benjamin Constant, whom we younger men have only seen rather *blasé*, exchanging his too inveterate habit of raillery for a slightly affected enthusiasm, a prodigiously amusing talker always, but whose wit was influenced by his other more powerful passions and faculties,—it was here at Coppet that he showed to the greatest advantage, proving himself to be, as Mme. de Staël uncontradicted has proclaimed, *le premier esprit du monde*, the greatest wit of the day: he was certainly the greatest of distinguished men. Their intellects were in accord; they always understood each other. Witnesses tell us that the sparkling brilliancy of their conversation in this chosen circle could not be surpassed; like a magic game of racket and ball, conversation was thrown from one to the other for hours without a single miss.

But we must not suppose that everybody there was always either sentimental or solemn; very often they were simply gay; Corinne had days of *abandon*, when she resembled the signora *Fantastici*. They often acted plays at Coppet, dramas and tragedies, or the chivalric plays of Voltaire, *Zaïre* and *Tancrède*, favourites of Mme. de Staël's; or plays composed expressly by her or her friends. These latter were sometimes printed at Paris, so that the parts might more easily be learned; the interest taken in such messages was very keen; and when in the interval some important correction was thought of, a courier was hurried off, and sometimes a second to catch him up, and modify the correction already *en route.* The poetry of Europe was represented at Coppet by many celebrated men. Zacharias Werner, one of the originators of that court, whose *Attila* and other dramas were played with a considerable addition of German ladies, wrote about this time (1809) to Counsellor Schneffer (we delete, however, two or three expressions to which the involuntarily sensual and voluptuous imagination of the poet is too apt): "Mme. de Staël is a queen, and all the intelligent men who live in her circle are unable to leave it, for she holds them by a magic spell. They are not all, as is foolishly believed in Germany, occupied in forming her literary character; on the contrary, they receive a social education at her hands. She possesses to admiration the secret of uniting the most unlikely elements, and all who come near her, however different their opinions may be, agree in adoring this idol. Mme. de Staël is of middling height, and, without possessing the elegance of a nymph, is of noble proportions. . . . She is healthy, a brunette, and her face is not exactly beautiful; but this is not observed, for at sight of her eyes all else is forgotten; they are superb; a great soul not only shines in them, but shoots forth flame and fire. And when, as so often happens, she speaks straight from her heart, we see how this noble heart is hedged round by all that is great and profound in her mind, and then one must adore her, as do my friends A. W. Schlegel and Benjamin Constant," etc.

It is not difficult to imagine to oneself the sprightly author of this picture. Werner, in his uncouth dress, purposely besmeared with snuff, furnished as he was with an enormous snuff-box, which he used plentifully during his long, erotic, and platonic digressions on *androgyne;* his fate was, he said, to be dragged hither and thither in fruitless search for that other half of himself, and from one attempt to another, from divorce after divorce, he never despaired of, in the end, reconstituting his original self. The Danish poet Œhlenschlæger* has given a detailed account of a visit he paid to Coppet, and he mentions the good Werner quite in this tone; we shall borrow from Œhlenschlæger's story a few other facts :—

"Mme. de Staël kindly came to me and invited me to spend some weeks at Coppet, joking me at the same time about my mistakes in French. I took refuge in German. She, and also her two children, understood that language well, and spoke it also very well. At Mme. de Staël's house, I met Benjamin Constant, August Schlegel, the old Baron Voght of Altona, Bonstetten of Geneva, the famous Simonde de Sismondi, and Count de Sabran, the only one of the company who did not know German. . . . Schlegel was, in my opinion, polite but cold. . . . Mme. de Staël was not pretty, but in the glance of her dark eyes there lay an irresistible charm; and she possessed in a high degree the gift of subduing obstinate natures, and by her own amiability drawing together men quite antipathetic to each other. She had a loud voice and rather a masculine face, but a delicate and tender heart. . . . She was then engaged on her *Allemagne*, and used to read a part of it to us every day. She has been accused of never having studied the books of which she speaks in this work, and is said to have been entirely submissive to the judgment of Schlegel. This is false. She read German with the greatest ease. Schlegel had, however, a certain influence over her, but she very frequently differed in opinion from him, and reproached him for his pre-

* Danish national poet; his first great poem was *Aladdin; or, The Wonderful Lamp.*—Tr.

judices. Schlegel, for whose learning and intellect I have a great respect, was in truth steeped in prejudice. He placed Calderon above Shakespeare; he severely criticised Luther and Herder. He was, like his brother, infatuated with the aristocracy. . . . If we add to all the virtues of Mme. de Staël that she was rich and generous, no one will be surprised to hear that she lived in her enchanted castle like a queen or a fairy; and her magic wand was perhaps that little twig which it was a servant's duty to place by her plate each morning, and with which she toyed during the conversation." Failing the laurel twig or the sacred mistletoe, it was her fan, an ivory or silver paper-cutter, or simply a morsel of paper, her fingers played with, — that hand impatient of a sceptre.

As for portraits of Mme. de Staël, we see how all who try to limn her agree in the chief points, from M. de Guibert to Œhlenschlæger and Werner. Two faithful and trustworthy portraits from the brush allow us to dispense with literary word-painting,— the portrait painted by Mme. Lebrun in 1807, which presents Mme. de Staël to us as Corinne, bare-headed, her hair in curls, a lyre in her hand; and the picture by Gerard, painted after her death, but from perfect, unerring remembrance. However, in collecting together several sketches from various contemporaneous pens, we think we have not done a useless thing; one is never weary of harmonizing many reminiscences of those beloved and admired ones who are no more.*

* One distinctive characteristic of the vast hospitality of Coppet was the order which reigned amidst so much variety and amusement; one enjoyed the ease of wealth without any of the profusion which causes the degeneration of many a brilliant life. Here a guiding hand made everything go smoothly, and by a wise economy of the means at hand,

English poetry, which, during the Continental wars, was unrepresented at this long congress of thought of which Coppet was the abiding-place, appeared there in 1816, in the persons of Lewis and Byron. The latter has spoken of Mme. de Staël in his Memoirs in an affectionate and admiring manner, despite a certain levity the *oracle* indulges in. *Blasé* as he is, he admits that she has made Coppet the most pleasant place in the world, through the society she chooses to receive there, and which her own talent animates. On her side, she pronounced him to be the most seductive man in England, always adding: "I credit him with just sufficient tenderness to destroy the happiness of a woman."*

But the inexpressible charm of Coppet during these its most brilliant years, that which you would now like to grasp, oh ye hearts, whether ye be still young

plenty of leisure was left for the enjoyment of romance and the drama ; the springs of household government were never visible, but all enjoyed the skilful result.

* About the same time that she expresses this opinion of Byron, she remarked, as if from some association of ideas: "I do not like B. Constant's book. I do not believe that all men are like Adolphe, but men are vain." From Byron's own Memoirs we read: "I send you *Adolphe* by B. C. ; it contains some painful truths, although in my opinion it is too sad a book ever to be popular. The first time I read it was in Switzerland (1816), by Mme. de Staël's desire ;" and he adds a contradiction of an erroneous supposition which had been spread. The original of Ellénore was Mme. Lindsay, she whom M. de Chateaubriand in his *Mémoires* calls the last of the *Ninons*. This, however, is no proof that more than one feature applicable to the author's *liaison* with Mme. de Staël may not have crept into the picture. These heroines of romance are very complex. Sismondi, however, has said too much about them in his Letters, since published ; and we are able to penetrate the mask better than is desirable.

and fresh, or disillusioned, rebellious of the present, passionately fond of the past, thirsting for an ideal which you no longer hope to find; oh, all you who are still, it has been justly said, what is best in the world after genius, inasmuch as ye have power to admire it, and with tearful eyes to feel it,—it is the seclusion, the interchange of thoughts and ideas among these guests beneath the leafy shades, and the noonday talks by the brink of these lovely waters clothed with verdure. A frequent guest at Coppet, knowing my deep interest (he is not one of those I have named above),[*] told me: "One morning I had come out of doors early to enjoy the fresh air. I lay on the thick grass by a pond in a remote part of the park, gazing dreamily at the blue sky. Suddenly I heard voices, two persons drawing near and nearer, talking. The conversation was loud and excited, and of a private nature. I tried to make a noise to warn them of my presence, and as I hesitated to get up, they came so near that it was too late to interrupt, and I was obliged to remain and hear everything—reproaches, explanations, promises,—unseen, and scarcely daring to breathe." —"Happy man!" I said; "and whose were the two voices? and what did you hear?" Then since the delicacy of the strolling guest evaded my questions, I was careful not to persist. Let us leave to romance, or to the poetic imagination of our descendants, the fresh colouring of such mysteries; we are still too close to them. Let time roll on, let the nimbus gather on these hills, let the hoary summits murmur forgetfully of long-past voices, and one day imagination can embellish at will the sorrows and the anguish of hearts in such hallowed Edens.

Corinne appeared in 1807. Its success was instan-

[*] I may now give his name,—he was Catruffo, the composer.

taneous and universal; but it is not from the criticisms of the press that we must prove this. Critical freedom, even literary criticism, had almost ceased to exist; Mme. de Staël about this time was not able to persuade the *Mercure* to insert a clever but simple analysis of the remarkable essay by M. Barante on the Eighteenth Century. When *Corinne* appeared, we were on the eve of, or threatened with, that absolute censorship. The sovereign's displeasure at the book,* probably because its ideal enthusiasm was not helpful to his aim, was sufficient to paralyse published praise. The *Publiciste*, always the moderate organ of M. Suard and of philosophic freedom in matters intellectual, had three good articles, signed "D. D.," which were probably written by Mlle. de Meulan (Mme. Guizot). On the other hand, M. de Feletz continued his curtly polite, but fault-finding, remarks in the *Débats*.†

* "If we are to believe an anecdote," says M. de Villemain in his beautiful studies on Mme. de Staël, "the ruler of France was so annoyed at the noise this romance made, that he himself wrote a critique for the *Moniteur*. He strongly censured the interest centred in Oswald, and characterized it as want of patriotism. Any one may read this clever and bitter criticism." I have tried in vain to find the article, which is probably not published under the direct heading of *Corinne*. I leave the pleasure of discovering it to those admirers of Napoleonic literature who are beginning to discover in their hero *the first writer of the century* (Thiers, Carrel, Hugo, etc.).—Render unto Cæsar the things that are Cæsar's, but do not lay all crowns at his feet.

† Since I had the honour of knowing this talented representative of the old art of criticism, I have better understood how much real goodness there was in him, and how his honest rectitude was consistent with those sharp, cutting remarks so trying to the *amour propre* of authors. When M. de Feletz had a grain of humour on his tongue, he could not help expressing it; his connection with journalistic criticism explains this. His

M. Boutard praised, and judiciously reserved his opinions in respect to art. One, "M. C." (whose name I do not know), had an article in the *Mercure* which was well intentioned but valueless. And what did all this continued criticism matter now to Mme. de Staël? With *Corinne*, her empire of fame was won. There is one decisive moment for genius, a moment in which it so firmly establishes itself, that for all time coming praise is interesting only to the vanity of those who bestow it. They are thankful to have the honour of commending, for so their names gain lustre in society, as a borrowed vase of gold will embellish our abode. Thus with Mme. de Staël; from the time *Corinne* appeared, Europe crowned her with the name she had immortalized. *Corinne* is the personification of the sovereign independence of genius at the very moment of its geatest oppression,—*Corinne*, who was crowned at Rome, in that Capitol of the Eternal City into which the conqueror who exiled her might not put his foot. Mme. Necker de Saussure (*Notice*), Benjamin Constant (*Mélanges*), M. J. Chénier (*Tableau de la Littérature*), have appreciatively analyzed the book, and have done so, so thoroughly that our task is curtailed. "*Corinne,*" says Chénier, "is *Delphine* still, but idealized and independent, giving free play to all her talents, and

mistake as regards his satire, which usually hit home, was that he did not recognise the grand and serious passages, and thus detracts from the effect. He wrote too purely for society, and never went deeply into anything; his jests also were carried too far, which made him seem unamiable. Mme. de Staël, who so seldom cherished resentment, made M. de Feletz the exception. On one occasion, when she observed him enter a salon, she went out by the other door. His crime was the only unpardonable one in her eyes: he had spoken ill of M. Necker. (See *Mélanges* by M. de Feletz, vol. vi. p. 280, and the volume subsequently published, *Judgments*, p. 352.)

always under the double inspiration of love and intellect." Yes; but for *Corinne* even glory is but a brilliant distraction, a grand opportunity to conquer hearts. "In seeking fame," she says to Oswald, "I have always hoped it would gain me love." The scheme of the book lays before us that struggle between nobly ambitious or sentimental faculties and domestic happiness, that perpetual aspiration of Mme. de Staël's. Corinne is simply resplendent at times as priestess of Apollo, while in the common relations of life we find her the simplest of women, gay, lively, with many charms, capable of the most gracious, unaffected *abandon*; but with all these attractions she is yet unable to escape from herself. From the moment passion touches her, when she feels herself seized *by that vulture's claw, beneath which happiness and independence sinks*, I love her helpless efforts to find comfort, I love her sentiment, which is more powerful than her genius, her ever recurrent invocations to the sanctity and continuity of the bonds which alone prevent sudden rendings asunder, and I love to hear her, in her dying hour, avow in her *chant du cygne* (swan-song): "Among all the faculties I owe to nature, grief alone is exhausted." This counterpart of *Delphine* which I find in *Corinne* is very seductive, and is the charm of the book to me. The severe situations in which this ardent, sensitive being is placed, are admirably calculated to enhance the picture. Lovers' names, not inscribed on the bark of some beech tree, but engraved on the eternal ruins, harmonize with the gravity of history, and become a living part of its immortality. The divine passion of a being whom we cannot believe to be only imaginary, introduces into the amphitheatre of antiquity one more victim who will never be forgotten; the genius which tore her away is another conqueror, and not the least, in that city of conquerors.

When Bernardin de Saint-Pierre was walking one day with Rousseau, he asked him if Saint-Preux was not himself: "No," replied Jean-Jacques, "Saint-Preux is not at all what I have been, but what I would like to have been." Almost all writers of poetic romance would speak thus. *Corinne* is what Mme. de Staël would have wished to be, and what, after all, except in the difference between the artistic grouping and her scattered life, she has been. She not only had the Capitol and the triumph of *Corinne;* she also had death through suffering.

That Rome, that Naples, which Mme. de Staël depicts in her own style in the poetic romance of *Corinne*, M. de Chateaubriand, about the same time, represents to us in his epic poem, *The Martyrs*. In this there is not the slightest interposing shade of German influence; with Eudore we go back to the simplicity of youth, while throughout we discern the masculine firmness of the design, the natural, spontaneous splendour of the glowing pen. For the comparison of all the different modes of feeling and of depicting Rome, since Rome began to be a city of ruins, we know nothing more complete than the shrewd and learned essay of M. Ampère.*

Rome, Rome! thy marbles and thy skies, vaster surroundings to lend support to less fleeting ideas! A talented woman once wrote: "How I love certain poems! It is with them as with Rome, all or nothing: we either live in them, or we cannot understand." *Corinne* is but an imposing variety of this worship of Rome, of this reverent power of entering in other epochs and with diverse minds, into the Eternal City.

* *Revue des Deux-Mondes*, 1835, vols. ii. and iii.

One delightful part of *Corinne*, and all the more charming because unusual, is the conversational style which is so often introduced, and the hankering after French society which the Count d'Erfeuil is made to express. Mme. de Staël mocks that too thoughtlessly witty society, but in such moments she is herself more French than she supposes: what she can express best, she, as it so often happens, disdains.

As in *Delphine*, there are portraits: Mme. d'Arbigny, that Frenchwoman who plans and calculates everything, is one, as is also Mme. de Vernon. It is privately whispered that she is Mme. de Flahaut, just as we also know the rather contrary individualities of which the noble figure of Oswald is a type, and as we recognise the truthfulness of the parting scene, and can almost realize the agony of Corinne during absence.

However, although in *Corinne* there are conversations and pictures of fashionable life, it is not, as regards this book just, to blame Mme. de Staël for incoherence or inconsistency of style, and for a degree of preference in the disposition of her ideas. For the general execution of this work she has quite abandoned the witty volubility which she sometimes indulged in (*stans pede in uno*) as she leant against the marble chimney-piece. If here and there incompleteness of style may be detected, it is only by rare accident; I have seen pencil jottings in a copy of *Corinne*, picking out the great number of *mais* (but), which give rather a monotonous effect to the first pages. Careful attention presides over every detail of this monument; the authoress has written in artistic, measured, and majestic language.*

* Heading a reprint of *Corinne* in 1839, we added: "Even as time passes, the interest which attaches to these works, once recognised as subsisting and durable, may vary, but is not less

The book on *Germany*, which appeared in London only in 1813, was on the eve of being published in Paris in 1810: the edition submitted to the imperial censors, Esménard and others, was completed, when, by the sudden tactics of the police, the sheets were sent to be waste paper, and the whole annihilated. The Duc de Rovigo's letter is well known; that disgraceful story is still fresh in our minds. Germany having become better known, and having besides made great advances since that time, Mme. de Staël's book may now seem less complete in the historical part; public opinion is, however, in these later times, more sensible in regard to such defects. But apart from the honour of initiating what no one else was capable of undertaking at the time, and which Villers alone, if he had had as much talent in writing as in conversation, could have divided with her, I do not believe that we could now find elsewhere such a vivid picture of that sudden birth of German genius, such a brilliant picture of that poetic age which may be called the century of Goethe; for the beautiful German poetry seems almost to have been great. Their very faults become characteristic of the description, and are not without their charm as the expression of a former taste which has given way to another, which in its turn will also pass away. Something has perished from the bosom of what continues to exist; that tinge of sadness is very appropriate in the midst of the admiration. It would be more suitable at this moment, when a recent mournful memory is associated with that immortal figure of Corinne, and when, our attention being drawn to Mme. de Staël, we involuntarily think of what the grave has but now taken from us. This book, which a father's death sent her to Italy to ponder over,—this book, scarcely thirty years old, has already seen her and her son and her daughter buried; it may well be read again in presence of these grave thoughts of death; for if it does not speak of the real mystery of the things of life, at all events we can extract from it nothing but what is generous, beautiful, and good."

born and to have died with that great man, and to have lived only the life of a patriarch; since then, there is already a falling off, a decadence.

In her introduction to *L'Allemagne*, Mme. de Staël lays great stress on the philosophical talent, on the nature of the doctrines as opposed to those of French ideology; at such moments she shows us that she is herself far enough from her earlier philosophy. Here (and let us carefully note this) we find indications of a growing anxiety for morality in her writings. A work is not in her opinion sufficiently moral unless it in some part aims at the perfectibility of the soul. In the admirable discussion which she makes Jean-Jacques carry on with a religious hermit, it is set forth that "genius ought only to manifest the supreme goodness of the soul." In some passages she appears very anxious to combat the idea of suicide. "When one is very young," she excellently says, "the degradation of existence being still unrealized, the tomb seems only poetic imagery, a sleep, and kneeling figures weeping round us; towards middle life it is no longer thus, and one understands then why religion, that science of the soul, has put the horror of murder along with the crime of suicide." Mme. de Staël, in the unfortunate position in which she was then placed, did not abjure enthusiasm, and her book closes with a glorification of it, although by the influence of religion she endeavours to restrain herself.

The *Essai sur le Suicide*, which appeared at Stockholm in 1812, was composed about 1800, and signs of a moral revolution in Mme. de Staël are there even more apparent than before.

The grief which the unexpected suppression of her book caused her was great. Six years of hopeful study wasted, and a redoubling of persecution at the moment when she had expected a truce ; other painful and contrary circumstances made her situation at this time both a violent crisis and a decisive ordeal, which ushered her into those unending years which I have called her darkest. Let it pass! let it pass! She is far beyond them now, there is henceforth nothing for her but glory which will never leave her ; there is neither position there, nor the chant of the Capitol. Till then the tempests of life had always left her a gracious reflex of light in these transitory allurements of fame,—to use her own charming expression, some *air ecossais* (Scotch melody) in her life. But from this time everything becomes more hard and bitter. First, youth—that grand and natural consoler—flies. Mme. de Staël had a perfect horror of age, of the idea of getting old ; one day, when she frankly expressed this sentiment before Mme. Suard, the latter said to her : " Never mind, you will get resigned to it, and be a very amiable old lady." But she shuddered at the thought : the word youth had a musical charm in her ears ; she loved to clothe her phrases with the sentiment of youth, and such simple words as *We were young then*, filled her eyes with tears. " Do we not often see," she exclaims (*Essai sur le Suicide*), "the spectacle of the torment of Mézence repeated by the union of a living soul with a ruined body, inseparable enemies ? What is the meaning of that sad *avant coureur* which nature causes to precede death, if it is not the order to exist without happiness, to abdicate daily, flower after flower in the crown of life ?" She kept herself behind as long as possible far from these *latter days which echo with hoarse voice the brilliant airs of youth*. The sentiment of which, at this time, she was the object on the part of M. Rocca, rather helped to increase her self-delusion in regard to youth ; she saw herself in the magic mirror of two young eyes blind to the ravages of years. But her marriage with M. Rocca, broken down by his wounds, the adoring love with which she gratefully devoted herself to him, her own impaired health, all inclined her for more home-like duties. *L'air ecossais, l'air brillant* of earlier times, became a grave hymn, holy and sad. From henceforth, religion breathed not only in her conversation, but in the practices of her daily life. When she was younger, less loaded with sorrow, it had sufficed for her to go in certain hours of sadness, to visit her father's tomb at the other side of the park, or with Benjamin Constant or M. de Montmorency, to engage in some deeply mystical conversation; as life advances, when courage is crushed by positive and increasing suffering, when all fails and fades day by day, and everything is colourless, passing inspirations are no support; we require a firmer belief, one more continually present with us : Mme. de Staël did not seek for it except where she could find it, in the gospel, in Christian religion. Before her complete conversion, her most critical time was during that long year which preceded her flight. The faithful constancy of some friends comforted her for the neglect, the cowardly excuses, the fear, disguised under the plea of ill-health, which others had hurt her by, wounding her heart in diverse ways. She felt herself surrounded by some contagion of fate, which affected all who were dearest to her ; her spirit rose to the danger. " *I am the exiled Orestes,*" she exclaimed to the intimate friends who were so devoted to her. And again : " In imagination I am in the tower of Ugolen.' Too much under restraint at Coppet, especially with her tormenting imagination, she longed with all her strength to enjoy a freer air, a larger space. The préfect of Geneva, M. Capelle, who had succeeded M. de Barante senior, pressed her to write something to celebrate the birthday of the king of Rome :* a few words would have smoothed all ways for her, opened every capital ; she did not think for a single instant ; in her well-known prompt reply she found nothing better to wish for the child than a good wet-nurse. The *Dix Années d'Exil* gives a natural description of the vicissitudes of that disturbed period ; she represents herself as ceaselessly studying the maps of Europe, regarded as the plan of a vast prison, which she was trying to escape from. Her earnest longing was towards England, but she would be obliged to reach it by St. Petersburg.

It was in this brooding disposition, and after that profound crisis resolved upon after mature thought, that the Restoration found Mme. de Staël, and brought her back (to France). She had seen Louis XVIII. in England. "We shall have," she announced then to a friend, " a king who will be a friend of literature." She liked this prince, whose moderate opinions reminded her of some of her father's. She was altogether converted to the political ideas of England, in that country which seemed to her the land of family life and public liberty. We see her returned from it appeased, soothed, no doubt full of the generous impetuosity which endured till her last day, but fixed in some half-aristocratic opinions, which from 1795 to 1802, she had by no means professed. Her hostility against the Empire, her absence from France, her association with the allied sovereigns and foreign society, the extreme craving for rest which impels the mind to take refuge in less daring impressions, — all these contributed to this metamorphosis in her. As she grew older, Mme. de Staël was very ready to reproach herself for some of her father's old ideas. Just so we have observed that character changes, and as people grow older they return

* Napoleon's son.—TR.

to the primitive type which distinguished them in childhood, casting off by degrees the formal habits contracted in the interval. It is the same in revolutions; after the outbreak, people fall back on more moderate demands, simpler aims than they at first thought of attaining, or of being contented with; and so we see Mme. de Staël towards the end of her life taking refuge in a more miscellaneous system, more temperate, and for her almost domestic: this, for the daughter of M. Necker, was simply returning to Saint-Ouen, accepting altogether the charter of Louis XVIII.

The *Considérations sur la Révolution française*, Mme. de Staël's last work, is the one which has established her fame, and which naturally classes her name in politics between the honoured names of her father and her son-in-law. It allows us to know her from a liberal point of view, Anglified, and rather *doctrinaire*, as they say, much better than we could otherwise have known her. Immediately after her return to France, she began to see in her own mind the unreasonableness of party spirit, and all the difficulties and complications which accompany restorations. Caution, and prudent, conciliatory measures were from the first indicated, counselled by her. In her connection with Mme. de Duras and M. de Chateaubriand, she sought to come to an understanding with the generous enlightened portion of a royalism keener than her own. " My system," she said in 1816, "is always absolutely opposed to that which is popular, and my most sincere affection is with those who follow it." She had from this time to suffer much and unceasingly in many of her private affections and relationships, which she had to sacrifice to the divergencies of opinion which arose; the cluster of human friendships relaxed and loosed around her; some new and precious acquaintances, like M. Mackintosh, only imperfectly compensated her. Painful days, but which come sooner or later in every existence, in which one sees the chosen ones who have been enfolded in the sacred shrine of an ideal love grow cool, then gloomy, one after the other, finding no pleasure in our society, failing altogether in that delicacy of affection which at first they showered on us! These inevitable disappointments, which the dearest friendships do not preclude, had a singular effect on Mme. de Staël, and weakened her hold, if not on life, at least on its vanities and perishable pleasures. She at last began to find less pleasure even in writing to M. de Montmorency, *l'admirable ami,* himself, on account of these unfortunate differences of opinion, to which he held too firmly. M. de Schlegel had a great grudge against this invading policy, and was less comfortable, or at times more sarcastic, in these troubled reunions, which no longer represented to him the delightful literary society of Coppet.

Mme. de Staël was quite sensible of this, and, already suffering from an increasing malady, consoled herself either in her family, or looking higher in *faithfulness to One who can never be unfaithful to us.* She died, however, surrounded by all those chosen friends whose names we love to see united with hers; she died in Paris,* in 1817, the 14th of July, on that day of liberty and sunshine, full of genius and sentiment, with undimmed faculties, and at a still early age. The evening before her death she made them wheel her chair into the garden, and distributed to those loved ones she was about to leave for ever, roses and blessed words of comfort as her last remembrances.

The posthumous publication of the *Considérations,* which took place in 1818, was a great event, and constituted for Mme. de Staël a brilliant political anni-

* Rue Neuve-des-Mathurins.

versary. In this work she suggests to the Revolution, and to the Restoration itself, a political interpretation destined to echo long, and to exercise an enduring influence. It was a monarchic *selon la Charte*, according to her. Outside this, and exclusive of M. de Chateaubriand's policy, safety was almost impossible for the Restoration: on the contrary, the harmony between these two extremes might possibly be prolonged indefinitely. Each faction, therefore, in the excitement of novelty, rushed to find in the book of *Considérations* weapons wherewith to defend its system. The praises were just, the censure passionate. Benjamin Constant in the *Minerve*, M. de Fitz-James in the *Conservateur*, wrote very strongly, and from very opposite points of view, as one may suppose. M. Bailleul and M. de Bonald wrote pamphlets on the work, each interpreting it in a contrary sense ; and there were many other pamphlets written on the subject. The thoughtful influence which through this work Mme. de Staël exercised on the younger liberal philosophical party, that which later on was represented by the *Globe*, was direct. The conciliatory, expansive, irresistible influence which would have resulted from her personal influence, was more than once much missed by the political party which, so to speak, emanated from her, and would have continued to be hers.

But it is in the domain of art that her influence would, I imagine, have been more and more delicately effective, cordial, intelligent, and untiringly encouraging to new talent, seeking it out, and moulding it with profit to itself and posterity. Among all those who at the present day are burning with unrecognised talent, scattered here and there, loose, unbound, she would perhaps have been a bond, the domestic hearth round which ideas could have been exchanged, enthusiasm rekindled; interpreting each other's thoughts, they would with her have perfected the union of art and imagination. Yes, if Mme. de Staël had lived, appreciative and sincerely affectionate as she was, how especially she would have delighted in that eminent woman's talent, which I cannot yet compare to hers! And after the publication of *Lélia*, how she would herself have hurried, full of tender dismay and indulgence, to comfort the authoress under the unfriendly severity and hypocritical morality of public criticism! Delphine, alone among all the women of the salon, went and sat by Mme. Récamier. Instead of vulgar curiosity or malicious flattery, how cordially she would have taken to her heart that womanly genius —more an artist than she herself, I grant, but so far less philosophic, less wise, less convinced, less deeply imbued with sound political views and quickened sensibilities! how she would have made her love life and glory! how eloquently she would have spoken to her of the *clemency of heaven*, and of the *beauty of the universe, which does not exist to defy man, but to typify for him a better life!* And lastly, how she would have praised her, and encouraged her to seek after more placid inspirations!

Oh you whom public opinion has already with one voice proclaimed first in the path of literature since Mme. de Staël, you have, I well know, in the admiration you display for her, a deep and tender gratitude for all the good she desired for you and may have done you! There will ever be in your glory an early bond which binds you to hers.*

* It will be understood that this refers to Mme. Sand. During the thirty years since this study of Mme. de Staël appeared (May 1835), many letters and documents have been published which have thrown more and more light on some of her ideas,

and made her better understood. I must content myself with drawing attention to the article on *Mme. de Staël, Ambassadrice*, published by M. Geoffroy in the *Revue des Deux-Mondes* of the 1st November 1856; the volume entitled *Coppet et Weimar*, published by Mme. Lenormant in 1862; a work the title of which is *La Comtesse d'Albany*, and the collection of *Lettres inédites* by Sismondi, published by M. Saint-René Taillandier in 1862 and 1863. But except for a few corrections in regard to details which might be added to our first idea, the essential and the principal features of the study which has just been read remain as true at this present time as they were thirty years ago. Let us guard against undoing, or even tainting, the worthy admirations, the well-grounded traditions of our youth.

JEANNE D'ARC.*

1850.

THE *Société de l'Histoire de France*, the labours of which have not been interrupted by the painful circumstances against which it has had to contend, has just completed a work of great national importance, the compilation of which had been entrusted to the painstaking and enthusiastic zeal of M. Jules Quicherat. This young and conscientious *savant* has collected and compiled, in five volumes, all the authentic documents which illustrate clearly the history of Jeanne d'Arc, particularly the full-length texts of the two lawsuits, the first called the *Procès de condamnation*, and the other the *Procès de réhabilitation*, which latter occurred twenty-five years later. The analysis of these proceedings, and the extracts from both documents, which had already appeared in various publications (especially in the *Collection des Mémoires*, edited by M. Michaud and M. Poujoulat), had attracted public attention; but extracts which give only the poetic and beautiful side of a question are very different from a literal reproduction of the exact purport of the Latin texts, and the so-called "instruments" of a voluminous legal procedure. We

* *Procès de Jeanne d'Arc*, published for the first time by M. J. Quicherat (6 vols. m. 8vo).

may say, indeed, that the memory of Jeanne d'Arc has been half buried in the dust of the recorder's office, from which it has only now been rescued. The compiler has been careful to quote, at the end of his work, testimonies from the historians and chroniclers of the time, regarding the Maid of Orleans, and he has also added some collateral articles which the careful student may like to see. So now we know all we shall ever learn regarding this marvellous being. As a finishing touch to his work, M. Quicherat has just added a separate and introductory volume, in which he gives modestly, but very precisely, his opinion on the new points which this complete development of the indictments in the *procès* brings out more clearly; it is a subject on which one is tempted to be led away by enthusiasm and legend, but we shall endeavour to be guided solely by love of truth.

Even after her death, the reputation of Jeanne d'Arc seems to have been subjected to every possible distortion; while within the circle of literary criticism, what sudden revolutions, what misadventures have befallen her! Chapelain's *La Pucelle* almost turned the heroine into ridicule; this poem, to quote the remark of M. Quicherat, was nearly as fatal to the memory of Jeanne d'Arc as a second verdict of condemnation would have been. It was so tedious that it incurred the cruel lash of Voltaire, who was the first to satirize this work, thereby gaining universal applause. It was then believed that such a subject could never again be treated seriously. It does not beseem us now to reproach Voltaire with a wrong so universally felt, and of which he himself would now be ashamed. Let us mention only that, in the eighteenth century, every one was charmed with this licentious *Pucelle*, and in my time the most decent people could recite long extracts from it; quite lately

I have heard some recited. We are told that M. de Maleshérbes himself knew his *Pucelle* by heart. Each century has these currents of contagious moral influence; they are unavoidable. Now we have passed to another extreme, and he would be a bold man who would venture to turn this subject into a vulgar jest. The present tendency, even if exaggerated, is, after all, infinitely more respectable; it is more true and more just, and I do not presume to condemn it.

From whatever point of view we may regard it, and however carefully we may guard ourselves against undue enthusiasm, we must admit the pathos of that figure, Jeanne d'Arc; no other in history is more worthy of pity and admiration. France, at the time she appeared, was at its lowest depths of misery. During fourteen years of war, which began by the disaster of Agincourt, nothing had occurred conducive to the moral elevation of the invaded country. The English king owned Paris; the Dauphin held his ground with difficulty on the Loire. One of his secretaries, Alain Chartier, who was one of the most able writers of his time, was among those who accompanied him. He has graphically described the state of distress, during which there was not a single place of refuge for any man of wealth and learning save behind the ramparts of a few cities. For "even the mention of the fields inspired one with a feeling of terror, and the country seemed to have become an ocean, where no other right but that of brute force predominated, and where each held possessions in proportion to his strength." It was at this time that, in a village situated in the valley of the Meuse, on the borders of Lorraine, a young girl, the daughter of simple, pious labourers, believed she heard a *voice*. She first heard this *voice* in her father's garden one day in

midsummer, when she was about thirteen years of age
(1425). She had fasted during the whole of the
previous day, nor had her fast been broken on that
morning. Thenceforth the voice continued to be heard
by her several times each week, very regularly, but
most frequently at particular hours, exhorting and
advising her. It counselled her to continue in good
behaviour, to attend church regularly, and to enter
France. The latter exhortation was continually repeated with great and still greater emphasis, and the
girl felt she could no longer remain at home. The
mysterious and solitary communications, and her
inward struggles, went on for two or three years.
Every fresh echo of her country's distress increased
her anguish. The *voice* never ceased to exhort her to
enter France at any price; and the exhortation became
even more impressive after the day on which the
English began the siege of Orleans,—that siege during
which every heart throbbed with the agony of suspense.
It commanded her to go instantly and raise the siege,
and when the child answered, "I am only a humble
girl, and know not how to ride or fight," the voice
responded, "It matters not—thou must go nevertheless."

This adventurous idea which tempted Jeanne had
become known, and was very displeasing to her father,
an honest, good-living man, who declared he would
rather see his daughter drowned than behold such
things. The voice gave Jeanne permission to disobey
the commands of her father, and, under the pretext of
visiting an uncle who lived in the neighbourhood, she
left her native village. She then induced this relative
to take her to Robert de Baudricourt, who was in
command at Vaucouleurs. At first Robert received
her rudely, roughly telling her that "her uncle should
box her ears and take her back to her father." But at

last, influenced by her determination to go in spite of all opposition, he yielded to her entreaties. She then insisted upon an interview with the Duke of Lorraine, who gave her some money. The inhabitants of Vaucouleurs themselves, full of interest on her behalf, undertook the expense of providing her with an equipment. Her uncle and a neighbour bought her a horse, the cost of which Robert de Baudricourt offered to reimburse. The latter, not without some soldier-like jests at the young girl's expense, as he helped her to mount, in her soldier's dress, wished her a safe journey to the Dauphin, saying, "Go, and come of it what may."

After a successful journey of eleven days, she found the Dauphin, who was then at Chinon (March 1429). Her public career now began, she being only seventeen years of age. Having made herself known to the king, and obtaining his consent, she resolutely followed the vocation that her faith in God and the mysterious voice prompted her to pursue; she told every one what had to be accomplished, and took command. At the end of April she reached the ramparts of Orleans; entered the town, and raised the siege, after a series of manœuvres that were very remarkable, according to the military tactics of those days. She appears to have been gifted with that peculiar promptitude of action which is a military intuition. The following months were filled with her victories and exploits,—Jargeau; Beaugency; the battle of Patay, where Talbot was made prisoner; Troyes, which she compelled to surrender to the king; Rheims, where she had him crowned,—four months of glorious success! Wounded before Paris on the 8th of September, fortune for the first time failed her, and the exhortations of the voice were for once misleading, or, at least, its counsels were rendered useless by the unwillingness and obstinate hesitation of her men. From this moment she had only flashes of success; her star had set, although neither her courage nor her devotion were extinguished. After divers mishaps and fruitless attempts, she was taken in a raid on Compiègne, the 20th May 1430, a little less than three months after her glorious appearance at Orleans. She was cast into prison, and given up by the Burgundians to the English, who in their turn consigned her to the mercy of the Inquisition. Jeanne's prosecution commenced at Rouen, in January 1431, and ended with the atrocious scene at the stake, where she was burnt alive, as a relapsed heretic, the 30th of May of the same year, being convicted of schism, idolatry, and witchcraft. She was then scarcely twenty years of age.

Now, are we not at once struck by this rapid transit of Jeanne d'Arc? do we not feel that life to her was but a momentary flash, as it nearly always is with beings so marvellously bright?

After our first impression of pity and admiration for this young and generous and innocent victim, we feel that, in order to admire her better, we must obtain a clearer insight into her character, and more fully realize her sincerity and the motives that prompted her to act; our thoughts go even beyond this, and we are inclined to ask ourselves, To what extent was her inspiration founded on truth? In short, the question resolves itself into this: Can we solve the mystery of Jeanne d'Arc by describing her as a natural being of great heroism and sublimity, who believed herself inspired, though really not otherwise than by human feelings? Or must we absolutely abandon the idea of obtaining any solution, unless by admitting, as she did herself, a supernatural intervention?

M. Quicherat's work gives us a clearer idea on this

subject, and provides us with nearly all the elements requisite for future treatment of this delicate question. Unluckily, an important paper is missing, and has never been found. If it existed, it would enable us to judge Jeanne in her true light, and give us a better insight into her early character. When Jeanne first came to Charles VII., he caused her to be interrogated and examined at Poictiers, in order to be convinced of her truthfulness and candour. It is this first simple statement, on the day of her arrival at the court, which would be of such inestimable value, because, though later on she answered the same questions before the judges who condemned her, she no longer spoke with the artless eloquence of that early deposition. However, in spite of this irreparable loss, we possess answers from her own lips which bear witness to her real condition from childhood. Without wishing to approach a question which entirely belongs to physiology and science, I will say only that the mere fact of habitually hearing voices, of believing what in reality are simply delusions to be spiritual manifestations, is a phenomenon, since proved in science, a rare phenomenon certainly, but one which does not constitute a miracle, nor does it necessarily constitute madness; it is absolute hallucination.

M. Quicherat very judiciously remarks : " In reviewing the evidence afforded by the documents, the idea I form of the Maiden of Domremy is that of a serious and religious child, endowed to the utmost with that intelligence peculiar to the superior beings of primitive society. She was nearly always alone, at church or in the fields, and became profoundly absorbed in communication with the saints whose images she contemplated." Her father's cottage was near the church. A little further, on an incline, was a spring called the *Currant Bush*, under a beech tree entitled the *Beautiful May*, the tree of the *Ladies* or *Fairies*. The belief in these fairies, to which Jeanne's judges attached so much importance, in order to convict her of intercourse with evil spirits, and whose names she scarcely knew, demonstrated, however, the idea of religious mystery with which this place was surrounded, and the atmosphere of vague fear and respect with which it was imbued. Further on was the *Oak Forest*, whence would proceed, according to tradition, a woman who would redeem the kingdom lost by a woman (Isabel of Bavaria). Jeanne knew this legend of the forest, and repeated it often, applying it to herself. On certain *fête* days the young village maidens assembled at the *tree of the fairies* with cakes and garlands of flowers to dance and play. Jeanne went with them, but not to dance ; and she often sat there alone indulging in secret dreams. But from the day the enemy brought murder and devastation into the valley, her inspiration became clearer. One idea emanated from her like an ardent prayer, and came to her again as an echo. The voice would speak to her as the voice of some superior being, a being distinct from herself, and whom, in her simplicity, she adored. The sublime and touching thought is that this humble girl's illusion was inspired by the vast pity she felt for her country and the persecuted Dauphin. Fostered by the ideas of the times, she had gradually accustomed herself to hear these voices, and to distinguish them as the voices of God's angels and of those saints who were dearest and best known to her. Her familiar angels were St. Michael and St. Gabriel ; and St. Catherine and St. Margaret were her counsellors. During her prosecution, on being questioned regarding the doctrine taught her by St. Michael—her principal guide and patron,—

she answered, that the angel, in order to arouse her, would relate the calamities that had befallen the kingdom of France.

Jeanne's inspiration came through her intense pity, not the pity of a woman who expends her feelings in tears, but the compassion of a heroine who feels that she has a mission, and who wields the sword to succour the unfortunate.

It seems to me that in history two distinct Jeannes have existed, who have been confounded one with the other, and it is difficult now to restore the first and original one. M. Quicherat's book gives us the key to the distinction. The original Jeanne is not quite like the heroine of tradition and legend; she is not so gentle or so demure, but she is truer and more energetic. When, twenty or twenty-five years after her condemnation, inquiries were made by Charles VII., in his somewhat tardy gratitude, the old witnesses were questioned, of whom a good number still existed. But these survivors were already under the influence of the universal legend, and were unable to reject it entirely in their statements. The majority appeared anxious not only to avenge the memory of Jeanne, but to idealize her, to show her off to advantage in every way, to represent her as the most blameless and exemplary of girls; and we can readily believe they have suppressed a good many characteristic points in her nature. For instance, there is a vast difference between the modest, gentle Jeanne and the one who is supposed to have jested with Captain Robert de Baudricourt, answering, in a somewhat off-hand way, respecting matrimony: "Yes—when I have accomplished all that God has commanded me, I shall have three sons— one of whom shall be a pope, one an emperor, one a king." This was but a playful war of words with the captain, and no doubt she only gave him his change, as one might say, and he replied like a real old soldier in similar tones.

When this girl of sixteen left her native village determined to win France, she was full of daring vigour both in word and action, though to a certain extent this quality failed her during her long months of imprisonment at Rouen. Her voice rang with light-hearted confidence. When she held neither a sword nor a banner she carried a bâton in her hand, according to the custom of the period, and this bâton she used for many purposes. "By my bâton I will make them bring provisions," she would swear, in speaking of the citizens of Orleans. This word bâton she continually made use of was, according to our best-informed historian, her ordinary oath. On hearing the worthy knight La Hire take the name of the Lord in vain, she reproved him, telling him to do as she did, and swear by his bâton. She was quite delighted, when informed by Dunois at the siege of Orleans, that an English troop, commanded by Falstoff, was approaching to bring help to the assailants; and, fearing not to be warned in time, so as to be prevented going, she exclaimed to Dunois: "Bastard, Bastard, in the name of God" (she may have said, "by my bâton," but probably the witness who stated this, considered the word too ignoble), "I command you, as soon as you learn that Falstoff has arrived, to let me know; should he come without your informing me, *I will have your head cut off.*" Even were this said only in jest, we see the kind of jest characteristic of the real Jeanne.

She is supposed to have had a horror of blood; and when asked by the judges which she preferred, the banner or the sword, she replied: "The banner, a thousand times. I carry the banner in the midst of

the enemy that I may not slay;" and, it is reported,
she never killed a single being. This evidence is very
explicit; it harmonizes with legend, with poetry, and
with the graceful statuette that a young and talented
princess has left of Jeanne d'Arc, representing her
stopping her horse at the first sight of a corpse. Jeanne
was not a Judith, nor can we suppose she was too
gentle or compassionate. She is said to have uttered
the following words: "At the sight of a Frenchman's
blood my heart stands still." But we must admit she
considered the blood of the English and Burgundians
to be of far less value. As a child she knew but one
Burgundian, and it would have delighted her to see his
head cut off, "*always supposing that it had been the wish
of God.*" According to the account of D'Aulon, her
steward, at the siege of Orleans, she was seen vigorously
attacking the enemy. After assailing the Bastille of St.
Loup, where there were about three hundred English-
men (others say one hundred and fifty), she planted
her banner on the edge of the trenches. The besieged
wished to surrender to her; but she refused to take
them at a ransom, crying, "I will capture you fairly."
She then ordered an attack, and *nearly every one was put
to death.* Speaking of a certain sword taken from a
Burgundian, she said she used it because it was an
excellent war sword and inflicted good cuffs and blows.
This would show that, if she did not *cut* or *thrust*, and
if she used the point as seldom as possible, she was
rather fond of striking with the flat side of the blade,
as she was wont to do with her bâton. I do not
mention this to detract in any way from the beauty of
the figure, but in order not to disguise her characteristic
vigour and frankness.

A young nobleman (Guy of Laval), who saw her at the
time of her glory, wrote of her to his mother, describing

her from head to foot. "I saw her mount her horse," he says, "arrayed entirely in an armour of white, with a small battle-axe in her hand. Her black steed had pranced and shied at the door of his stable, and would not let her mount. 'Lead him to the cross,' she said. This cross was near the church, by the road-side. On seeing the cross, the horse became tractable, and she was able to mount him." The young narrator saw a miracle in this occurrence. All narrators and eye-witnesses of that period come to the same conclusion in speaking of her, and the most minute and natural incidents appear to them miracles. "Once on her steed, the maiden," continues Guy of Laval, "turned to the door of the church, and exclaimed, in her clear, feminine voice, 'Ye priests and people of the church, make your processions, offer up your prayers to God;' then she went on her way, crying, 'Forward! forward!' A graceful page marched before her, bearing a furled banner, while in her hand she held her battle-axe."

This is a picture of Jeanne in all her military grace and beauty, speaking in a woman's voice, though in tones of command, whether addressing her pages, or giving orders to the clergy.

We do not doubt that the day after the siege of Orleans, she may have had a moment of wild exaltation. In the fulness of her accomplished mission, she was tempted to say, like all visionaries, "I am God's voice." She wrote to the towns, commanding them to open their gates to the Maid of Orleans; and she thus issued her commands to the Dukes of Bedford and Burgundy: "In the name of the King of Heaven, my Guide and Sovereign Saviour:" When, afterwards, in cooler moments, her letters were shown to her in prison, she had difficulty in recognising them, though there is no doubt they were thus dictated by her. She wrote to

K

the heretics of Bohemia, exhorting them to return to their duty: "I, the Maiden Jeanne, to tell you the real truth, would have overtaken you long ago with my avenging arm, had not the war with the English detained me here. But should I not soon hear of your amendment, your return to the bosom of the Church, I may perhaps leave the English and turn against you, to extirpate your frightful superstitions." Probably the style was that of her secretary, but the ideas must certainly have been her own. The Count of Armagnac wrote to her from the confines of Spain to ask which of the three popes then reigning was the legitimate one. She answered: "I am too much taken up with the war to satisfy you at once. But when you know I am in Paris, send me a message, and I will then tell you truthfully in whom you should believe, and all I shall have learnt concerning this matter, through the counsel of my Guide and Sovereign Saviour, the King of the whole world." Such letters as these, produced during the prosecution, strongly supported the accusation brought against her, of having attempted to usurp the functions of the angels of God and His ministers on this earth. It appears certain that, however unfavourable fortune might have been to her, she would have ventured further still, with the counsel of her voices; and that she did not consider herself merely destined to raise the siege of Orleans and to accomplish the coronation at Rheims. The young and ardent soul would readily have entered on a wider field; and there, again, I fancy I perceive the primitive Jeanne d'Arc possessed by a Demon or Genius (whatever you like to call it), but a Genius in the garb of that period; the natural Maid of Orleans, with no undue softness about her—bright, proud, rather rough, swearing by her bâton, and using it when necessary; a little intoxicated by the success of her mission; full of confidence in her own powers, exclaiming, "I am the voice of God;" speaking and writing in the name of God to the princes, lords, and citizens of the different towns, and to heretics in foreign countries; inclined, too, to go into questions of orthodoxy and Christianity, if only allowed leisure to listen to her voices. Already the people, in their extreme devotion, urged her on in her convictions; they were predisposed to believe in her, to reverently render her their devoted homage. But alas for her great and glorious career, which she was able only to rough-hew, for she hardly gained a glimpse of it during the few months of her triumph, and this is not to be regretted; it is in the peculiar heroism of her mission that she is so touching and sublime. Her contemporaries felt this after her death. Therefore, nearly all those in her favour (and all were more or less so in the *procès de rehabilitation*) cling to the belief that she never professed to be destined to perform more than the special acts of raising the siege of Orleans, and conducting the king to Rheims; consequently, she accomplished all that the voices told her. This is an illusion of the national imagination, which would like to render Jeanne infallible. But we have positive evidence that her voices promised much more from her than she would perform, and in her death-agony, her faith and supreme confidence in God must have been great to enable her to exclaim, in the midst of the flames, "My voices have not, after all, misled me!"

In emphasizing the energetic and somewhat rough characteristics of the noble shepherdess, far be it from me to deny her the quality of gentleness, a gentleness all the more deep and true that it was not excessive. During the march from Rheims to Paris (August 1429), as she was arriving with the king from the neighbourhood of La Ferté-Milon and Crépy-en-Valois, the people came out in crowds to meet her, crying *Noël*.* Jeanne, who was riding between the Archbishop of Rheims and the Count Dunois, remarked, " These are good people; I have never seen any so glad to welcome the arrival of such a noble king. God grant that when I end my days I may be buried in their midst." To which the Archbishop replied, " Jeanne, where do you hope to die?" She replied, "Wherever it shall please God, for I am not more certain of time and place than you are yourselves; and may it please my Creator to let me, retire now from warfare to serve my father and mother in tending their sheep."· Here we see the real gentleness of Jeanne's nature after her momentary enthusiasm, when the excitement of war had passed.

It is superfluous to say she was perfectly chaste; all witnesses are unanimous on this point. The old Squire Bertrand de Poulengy, who in his youth had the honour of escorting Jeanne from Vaucouleurs to Chinon, and the Duke d'Alençon, her favourite among all the captains, both testify strongly that, notwithstanding the dangers of close companionship, no immodest thought ever shadowed the purity of her simple, modest virtue.

The judges who condemned her were insulting, and the Bishop of Beauvais, who conducted the case, united the most consummate craft with his brutality. But that which is the most striking in these days, when we read the entire procedure, is the outrageous materialism of those theological practitioners, who understood nothing of Jeanne's vivid inspiration, who in all their questions strove to debase her elevated and simple meaning, though they were unable to render it coarse. They appeared, above all, extremely anxious

*. A popular exclamation of delight, used at that time by the French people in welcoming a sovereign.—TR.

to ascertain under what form she had seen St. Michael. "Did he wear a crown? Had he any clothes? Was he not entirely naked?" To which Jeanne replied, much to their discomfiture, "Do you think that God could not clothe him?" They always returned to this foolish question. She at last silenced them by saying, "He appeared to me in the form and vesture of a truly honest man." Once, at Poictiers, during the early days of her arrival at court, when one of the doctors of the place wished to know absolutely from her what kind of dialect the Archangel used in addressing her, she answered the provincial doctor, "He speaks much better French than you do." It is remarkable that the *procès* of condemnation, organized with the object of dishonouring the memory of Jeanne, has been rather the means of sustaining it. We are inclined to think with M. Quicherat that, though carried on by the judges and her enemies, it redounds more to the honour of the real Jeanne d'Arc, is more conducive to our full understanding of her life, more trustworthy in all that concerns her, than the *procès de réhabilitation*, already to some extent tainted by idle legend. Jeanne's finest sayings, her most simple, true, and heroic words, have been recorded by the judges, who have handed them down to us. This *procès* was much more *en règle* (according to the inquisitorial law then in force) than has since been believed, though it was none the less odious and execrable. But these judges, like all the Pharisees of the world, like those who condemned Socrates, like those who condemned Jesus, did not thoroughly know what they were doing, and their authentically written exposition of the case forms the immortal and avenging gospel of the victim.

Those judges, anxious to convict her of idolatry, questioned her incessantly about the picture on her banner, whether she did not think that such a banner possessed magical power. To which she replied, that her only magic lay in the following words addressed to her men : "Throw yourselves boldly among the English ; I shall lead you on !" She was severely censured for having had the same banner conveyed to the church at Rheims for the coronation, in preference to any other. Her answer was the following oft-quoted speech : " It had been all through the misery, it. was but right it should also have the glory and honour."

There is an admirable passage in Homer. Hector having driven the Greeks from the walls of Troy, is on his way to besiege them in their camps, and attack their retrenchments, determined also to set their ships on fire ; when suddenly a miracle takes place. An eagle appears in the sky, grasping between its claws a serpent, which, mutilated as it is, tears open the breast of its imperious enemy, forcing it to relinquish its hold. At this sight, a certain Trojan (Polydamas by name), wise in omens, approaches Hector, and, after interpreting the sign to him, advises him to relinquish the field that he already considers his own. At these words, Hector is furious, and threatens to pierce Polydamas with his lance, saying, " It matters little to me what the birds portend ! My orders come direct from mighty Jupiter, the only god whose will is omnipotent. There is but one supreme augury, and that is, fight for one's country."

In the attack upon Paris, which occurred the 8th of September (a festival in honour of the Nativity of Our Lady), Jeanne was wounded, and this was the end of her success. This ordering of the attack on a festival of the Church was made a chief point against her ; the doctors and judges accused her of irreverence and lack of religious devotion. In questioning her, they said,

"You knew it was a Church festival, was it right on your part to fight on such a day?" She eluded further questions on the subject, and answered, with downcast eyes, "Pass on to something else."

The noble girl, thus in the serpent's coils, dared not answer like Hector, though she thought as he did. Like him, she had direct commands from the Almighty God. What mattered other auguries to her! Direct inspiration gave her faith and strength; yet this very inspiration was a crime in the eyes of her judges. She had firm belief in the reality of her *voices*, and, like all visionaries, she believed she drew her inspiration from its very source, from the Holy Spirit of God. The ecclesiastical order, the Church, organized as it was in these days, appeared to her to be probably worthy of respect, but her voices held the first place in her consideration. She felt that she possessed the moral power to command both priests and churchmen, to rouse them and lead them back to the right path, just as she had led princes and captains. Therefore, in the *procès de réhabilitation*, we do not find that Rome was so eager or so well-disposed as might have been imagined. The king was obliged to put pressure on the pope; and Jeanne, who had every qualification for being canonized, was never more than the saint of the people and of France.

Historians understand her at last; they present the simple maiden in a proper light, and we cannot help recalling to our remembrance what M. Michelet says in vol. v. of his *Histoire de France*. Nevertheless, a severely precise criticism might detect many errors and deviations from the exact truth in that brilliantly written sketch. The author, as usual, strives after effect, he forces his colouring, he makes mere buffoons of the intervening characters, trifles in the wrong places, adopts an unnatural gaiety and smartness, and is too dramatic and fond of metaphor. The impression he leaves with one, of the *procès*, does not agree with the original interrogatories, which are much more grave and simple. With these reservations, however, we must admit that M. Michelet has grasped the spirit of the chief personage, that he has vividly pourtrayed the impulsive excitement of the populace, the shouts of enthusiasm, which, truer and more powerful than any set doctrine, rose in honour of the noble maiden,—an enthusiasm which, in spite of Chapelain and Voltaire, has enshrined her ever since. The Jeanne d'Arc of M. Michelet is truer than any former one.

There remains, I believe, in the volumes just published by M. Quicherat, yet another Jeanne d'Arc to discover, a heroine so skilfully yet simply pourtrayed, that she must satisfy every generously reasonable mind. Even should philosophical criticism find that there are some inexplicable points which can never be reconciled, I do not consider this a very grave misfortune. Shakespeare's Hamlet admirably says, "There are more things in heaven and earth than are dreamt of in our philosophy." If we read M. Quicherat's volumes attentively, and take into consideration the difficulties he himself admits, I do not think it will be impossible, after such careful and unprejudiced study, to evolve from them a Jeanne d'Arc at once sincere, sublime, and unpretending.

MARIE ANTOINETTE.

1851.

AMONG all the books and papers which may happen to give a correct idea of Queen Marie Antoinette, and of her character in her youthful years of prosperity, I do not know any which better convinces the reader's mind, than the simple notes from the Comte de La Marck's diary, inserted by M. Bacourt into the introduction of the work he has recently published on Mirabeau. In a few clearly expressed pages, the Comte de La Marck reveals to us the true character of the Queen; in them we find a Marie Antoinette real and natural, and not overdrawn in any way. We anticipate the faults to which her surroundings will not fail to impel her, those which will be attributed to her, and the weapons which unwittingly she will furnish to the malice of her enemies. It is to be regretted that such an impartial and skilful observer did not draw a like portrait of the Queen, at different stages of her life, up to the supreme hour of her immolation, when all the noble qualities and virtues of her heart were so courageously revealed, that they must interest and impress every human being.

It is a way of approaching Marie Antoinette which to me appears just, and which I would wish to define, because I consider that all historical judgment should be concluded from the same data. From a feeling born of compassion, some are charmed into an ideal interest in Marie Antoinette; they wish to defend her from all attacks, constitute themselves her advocates, her knights-errant; are indignant at the mere idea of faults and weaknesses which others think they discover in her life. This *rôle* of defender is highly honourable if it is sincere; it is easily to be conceived as existing among those with whom the old order of royalty is a creed, but among the newer, modern-minded men, it impresses me less, as I doubt its sincerity. Such views and feelings are not mine; they can scarcely be the views and feelings of men who have not to any great extent been educated in the tradition of the old monarchy, and this we cannot deny to be the case with the great majority of the present and also of the coming generation. What appears to me the safest course, and the most desirable, for that touching memory of Marie Antoinette, is to try to detach from the great heap of writings and testimonies, of which she has been the subject, the beautiful, noble, gracious figure, with all its weaknesses, frivolities, frailties perhaps,—but with all its essential good qualities preserved and acknowledged in their integrity; the virtues of wife, mother, and, at certain moments, of queen, kind-hearted and generous at all times, and finally displaying the merits of resignation, courage, and sweetness, which crown great misfortunes. When such a fair and even judgment is once historically established, she will continue, through all the ages, to excite the interest of those who, becoming more and more indifferent to the politics of the past, will still cherish those delicate and humane sentiments which are a part of civilisation, and the source of that sympathy which, weeping over the misfortunes of Hecuba and Andromache, will deplore her similar but greater miseries.

But there is this difference, that poetry alone is responsible for the tradition of Andromache and Hecuba, and we have no memoirs of the court of Priam, whilst we do possess those of the court of Louis the XVI., and by no means can they be ignored. And what do those memoirs say of Marie Antoinette? I speak of faithful, not of libellous memoirs. What says the Comte de La Marck, who sums up very ably the spirit of that earlier time?

Fifteen when she arrived in France, the young Dauphiness was not nineteen when she found herself the Queen of Louis XVI. This prince had received solid instruction, and was endowed with good moral principles, as we know; but he was feeble, timid, brusque, and rude, and particularly ungracious towards women, possessing none of the qualities necessary to direct and guide a young wife. She, the daughter of an illustrious mother, Marie Thérèse, had in her early training at Vienna been sadly neglected, as her mother was too much occupied with State affairs to superintend the education of her daughter. No one had ever tried to cultivate in her mind a taste for serious reading; so, although she was by no means deficient in intelligence, and "quickly grasped and understood things told her," she had no great capacity; and, in fact, was too indolent to repair the defects of education, and the want of experience. Amiable, gay, and full of innocent fun, she was especially kind-hearted, and always anxious to oblige any one who appealed to her. She had a great craving for intimate friendship, and immediately sought some closer acquaintanceship than is usual in courts. Her idea of happiness (we each form our own) was to escape from ceremonial, which wearied her, and to create for herself a little world of kindly, happy, devoted, chosen followers, among whom, to outward seeming, she forgot that she was a queen, although in reality her royal dignity was not forgotten. She loved, so to speak, to give herself the pleasure of this oblivion, not to recall her own identity till some opportunity arose for showering good gifts around her; just as, in pastorals and comic operas, we have seen disguised queens who in this way charm and delight all who surround them. Marie Antoinette might have been able to realize this ideal life without any inconvenience, had she remained a simple arch-duchess at Vienna, or had she reigned over some small domain like Tuscany or Lorraine. But in France this kind of life could not be tried with the same freedom; and her *Petit Trianon*, with its dairies, its sheep-folds, and its comedies, was too near Versailles; Envy prowled around those favoured spots, Envy beckoning on Calumny and Slander.

M. de La Marck has shown us how injudicious it was on the part of the Queen to confine herself so exclusively to the circle of the Comtesse Jules de Polignac, to confer on her, along with the position of a friend, the appearance of a favourite; and to allow all the men of that coterie (men like Vaudreuil, Besenval, and Adhémar) to assume pretensions and privileges, which each, according to his disposition or ambition, so quickly abused. Although she never understood the full extent of this inexpediency, she did perceive it to some extent; and began to feel that where she sought to find repose and refreshment, and relaxation from the duties of exalted rank, she was still beset by importunity; and when some one remarked to her that she showed too great a preference for the distinguished strangers who sojourned in France, and that this was prejudicial to her own popularity among the French people, she replied sadly, "You are right, but they at least ask me for nothing."

Some of those men thus admitted to the intimate favour of the Queen, and bound by gratitude and respect, were the first to speak lightly of her, because they did not find her submissive enough to their aims. When on one occasion she seemed to withdraw a little from the Polignac circle, and to frequent oftener the salon of Mme. d'Ossun, her lady of the bedchamber, a *habitué* of the Polignac circle (whom M. de La Marck does not name, but who seems to have been an important member of the circle), composed a very wicked couplet against the Queen ; and this couplet, founded on an infamous lie, was soon circulated in Paris. Thus did even the Court and the Queen's intimate circle furnish the first leaven which was to mingle with the coarseness and infamy of the outside world. As for the Queen herself, she knew nothing of what was going on, and never suspected the cause of her disfavour at Versailles, any more than of her estrangement in Paris.

Even at the present day, if we wish to quote some testimony against Marie Antoinette, we go to the Memoirs of the Baron de Besenval to find it. Ordered to appear before the Queen in 1778, at the time of the duel between the Comte d'Artois and the Duc de Bourbon, M. de Besenval was introduced by Campan (the private secretary) into a secret room which he had not known of before, "simply but conveniently furnished. I was astonished," he added, "not that the Queen required so many facilities, but that she had dared to procure them." This phrase spread abroad, was suggestive, and enemies were not wanting to take it up.

We now approach the most delicate part of the subject, and as I am not afraid, I shall not affect more reticence than is necessary. There are persons who are most anxious to deny absolutely all levity, and all heart weakness, on the part of Marie Antoinette. But, assuming that either were apparent at this time of her life, for my part I boldly affirm that the interest attached to her memory, the pity which her misfortunes and her noble manner of bearing them excites, the execration which her judges and jailors deserve, must in no way depend on any discovery relating to former womanly weaknesses, nor be in the smallest degree invalidated by such a discovery. Now, taking into account all our actual historical information and trustworthy testimony regarding Marie Antoinette, and remembering also what we have been told by well-informed contemporaries, it is quite permissible to suppose that this young creature, with all her lively, tender feelings, ready to be impressed by elegant manners and chivalrous attentions, craving for sympathy and support, had, during her youth, some preference; it would be the contrary rather which would be strange. Many ambitious men, many coxcombs, tried to gain her good graces, and were disappointed; the innumerable attempts had only beginnings. We heard Lauzun the other day describe his adventure; but although he tells his story in his own way, he breaks down. The Prince de Ligne often came to France at this time, and was one of those strangers, altogether French and altogether agreeable, with whom the Queen was particularly well pleased. He had the honour of accompanying the Queen in her morning rides. "It was," he says, "in such rides alone with the Queen, although accompanied by her brilliant royal escort, that she told me a thousand interesting anecdotes concerning herself, and all the traps which had been laid to give her a lover. At one time it was the house of Noailles which wished her to take the Vicomte; at another, the Choiseul faction destined Biron (Lauzun) for her. La Duchesse de Duras, when it was her week to be in attendance, accompanied us in our rides, but we left her with the equerries; and this was one of the Queen's blunders, one of her greatest crimes, since she never committed any other, that bores and tiresome persons, who are always implacable in their resentment, considered themselves neglected." So this is the Queen's version of Lauzun's story: I would always have it remembered, that it is improbable that Lauzun acted for the Choiseul faction, with whom he was never on good terms; but it was the interest of the Queen's *entourage* to present him in this light to ruin him definitely. It was this same Prince de Ligne who elsewhere said of the Queen, "her pretended gallantry was never anything more than deep friendship, with which she distinguished *one* or *two* persons" (I retain his style of Grand Seigneur), "and the womanly coquetry natural in a young Queen who desired to please everybody." This impression, or conjecture, which I find shared by other keen observers who have written of Marie Antoinette, is, I believe, most likely to be correct. The *two* persons whom she so particularly distinguished at different times, appear to have been, first, the Duc de Coigny, a sensible, prudent man of mature years; and, secondly, M. de Fersen, colonel in the regiment of Swedish Guards in the service of France, a man of high character and chivalrous nature, who, in days of misfortune, betrayed himself only by his absolute devotion.

Now, when we discuss matters of such very peculiar and intimate secrecy, matters about which it is so very easy to form many suppositions, and so difficult to acquire any certain knowledge, I think it well to recall to mind the apt expression of Mme. de Lassay (the illegitimate daughter of a Condé), who, when she heard her husband discussing very plainly the virtue of Mme. de Maintenon, looked at him with amazement, and with admirable coolness remarked, "What did you do, monsieur, that you seem so perfectly sure about matters of that kind?" The remark, which was very sharp from a wife to a husband, who challenged it by his claim of authoritative judge of disputed virtue, is true in other senses, and might with equal justice be addressed to those who are so sure of the errors of others, even when those errors had no witnesses.

The beauty of the Queen in her youth is famous, although it was not the kind of beauty where each feature might be examined and criticised apart; her eyes, although expressive, were not very beautiful; her aquiline nose was perhaps too pronounced. "I am not quite sure that her nose really ought to have belonged to her face," said one witty observer. Her lower lip was thicker than we care for in a beautiful woman, her figure was also a little too full; but the whole was a beautiful woman, with an air of noble dignity. Even in *déshabille* it was a regal beauty rather than the beauty of a woman of the world. "No woman," said M. de Meilhan, "carried her head better; it seemed poised so perfectly that each of her movements was full of grace and majesty. Her carriage was noble, her step light and firm, and recalled the expression of Virgil, *Incessu patuit dea*. The most uncommon thing about her, was a most imposing union of grace and dignity." Add a complexion of dazzling whiteness, lovely hands and arms, a charming smile, a winning gift of language which expressed more heart than wit, and showed her desire to please and to be pleased. She could enjoy and permit, as she liked, liberty of speech, and freedom from restraint in pleasures and amusements; she could play at being a shepherdess or a woman of the world, for she had only to rise up, and with one little motion of her head she was at once the Queen.

For a long time the gracious woman, secure in the prestige of her royal dignity, and thinking only of tempering with kindness the etiquette which surrounded her, paid no attention to politics; or, if she did, it was only incidentally, or when, in a manner, forced to it by the advice of her intimates. She continued her life of fairy-like illusion, while already odious reports, satirical couplets, and infamous pamphlets were circulating in Paris, imputing to her a systematic, secret influence which she had not assumed. The Collier affair was the first signal of misfortune; the bandage, which till then had covered her eyes, was torn off. She began to emerge from her enchanted hamlet, and to discover the world as it is when it has a mind to be wicked. When she was at length persuaded to interest herself habitually in politics, and to form opinions of her own on the extraordinary events which day by day enforced attention, she brought the most unpolitical mind imaginable to bear upon them; I mean indignation against acts of baseness and personal prejudices, which, being very evident, did not always help to make her cause triumph; resentment of wrong which did not declare itself in any desire for vengeance, but rather by the delicate and proud forbearance of wounded dignity. If Louis XVI. had been different, if he had yielded to any impulse of active energy, there is no doubt that at one moment or another, under the inspiration of the Queen, he would have attempted some enterprise, which might probably have been a rash deed, but which, on the other hand, might probably have established firmly, for a time, the disturbed order of monarchy. But he did not do this;

it was the character of Louis XVI. which failed, and through his very virtues he disappeared from his *rôle* of king; his nature, a compound of piety and human weakness, even bent towards self-sacrifice, and as his character became gradually weaker and weaker, he could have recovered his greatness only by becoming a martyr. The Queen had not power to triumph over this royal indolence and incapacity; she did make several attempts, but was not persistent enough. This is the ever-recurring plaint which issues from the pen of the Comte de La Marck, in the secret correspondence which is just published. "The Queen," he writes to the Comte de Mercy-Argenteau (30th December 1790), "the Queen certainly possesses strength of mind, and sufficient firmness to enable her to do great things; but it must be confessed, and you have had better opportunities of remarking it than I have had, that, be it on business affairs, or simply in ordinary conversation, she does not always display that amount of attention and perseverance which are necessary for the thorough understanding of what one ought to know to prevent mistakes and to ensure success." And elsewhere we find from the same to the same: "I must speak out, the King is incapable of reigning; and the Queen, well seconded, might alone make good this incapacity. But even this would not be enough; it would be more than ever necessary for the Queen to recognise the need of applying herself to business with method and persevering attention; she would have to make it a rule with herself not to make half-confidences to several people, but, instead, to give her whole confidence to whoever she might choose to second her." And again, on the 10th of October 1791: "The Queen, with some intelligence and courage, which has been proved, still allows all the occasions on which she might seize the reins of government, to escape her; and continues to surround the King with faithful people, devoted to her service, and to the salvation of the State, by her and through her. A long-continued habit of frivolous thoughtlessness cannot be thrown off in a day; it would have been more like the genius of a Catherine of Russia to struggle against such unforeseen dangers and difficulties, than of one who, like Marie Antoinette, had never opened a book of history in her life, and had dreamt only of royal indolence and of village leisure at Trianon; it is enough that this past frivolity had in no degree degraded or soiled the heart, which was proved to be as generous, as proud, as loyal, and as nobly gifted, as if it had come straight from nature's hand."

I shall not, as may be well supposed, dispute the line of politics to which Marie Antoinette thought it best to return when she was left to herself. We are not constitutional purists; what she wished was certainly not the constitution of '91, it was the salvation of the throne, the salvation of France, as she believed, the honour of the king, and her own honour, and that of her nobility, the integrity of the heritage which would be her children's; do not expect anything else from her. Those of her letters which have been already published, and others which will one day be published, will allow this portion of history to be established with certainty.

She desired the safety of the State, through her brother, the Emperor, or through some other powerful foreign aid, but not by the aid of the *émigrés*, against whom she could not restrain her indignation. "The cowards, after having abandoned us," she exclaimed, "would exact that we run all the risks, and serve their interests." In an excellent letter which she wrote to the Comte de Mercy-Argenteau, we find her saying, after disclosing a desperate plan, "I have listened, as attentively as I could, to people of both sides, and from the advice of both I have formed my own opinion; I do not know if my advice will be followed, you know with whom I have to deal" (the king); "the moment one believes him to be persuaded, a word, an argument, makes him change before you can suspect it; this is also the reason why so many things cannot be attempted. Now, whatever happens, let me retain your friendship and attachment, I have much need of such support; and believe that, whatever may be the misfortune which pursues me, I may yield to circumstances, but I shall never consent to anything unworthy of myself; it is in misfortune that I feel most who I am. My blood flows in the veins of my son, and I hope that one day he will show himself worthy of being the grandson of Marie Thérèse."

Her last gleam of joy and hope was the journey to Varennes. When this oft-delayed journey was at last about to be accomplished, towards midnight the Queen was crossing the Place du Carrousel, on foot, to reach the carriage prepared for the royal family by M. de Fersen, when she was met by the passing carriage of M. de La Fayette; she observed it, "and she had the spirit, even at such a moment, to try to strike the wheels of this carriage with a little cane she carried in her hand." It was an innocent revenge, and that little switch with her cane may be called her last act of playfulness. Three days later, how the aspect of affairs had changed. The instant Mme. Campan came into her presence, after the return from Varennes, the Queen, uncovering her head, told her to behold the effect grief had produced on her hair; "in one single night it had turned as white as the hair of a woman of seventy, and she was thirty-six."

The two last years of the Queen's life would redeem

a thousand times as many faults as this gracious lady
could have committed in her thoughtless years, and
must perpetuate through all time a reverend pity for
her sad fate. A prisoner in her own palace, a prey
to constant agony of mind, we see her nature being
purified day by day, beside that sainted sister, Mme.
Elizabeth, her principles and her affections fortified and
concentrated, to such an extent as would have been impossible had her heart not been naturally good and true
and incorrupt. On those fatal days of riot and insur-
rection, when even her private apartments were invaded,
she remained firm at her post of duty ; she bore the outrage proudly, nobly, even with gentle indulgence, whilst
with her own body she protected her children. In the
midst of her own peril, she was, in her tender goodness,
only troubled about others, and she showed herself
most careful not to compromise needlessly those interested in her cause. On that last day, the supreme
day of royalty, the 10th of August, she made one last
attempt to inspire Louis XVI. with the courage which
would have made him die a king, a worthy son of
Louis XIV. ; but Louis was to die a Christian, the son
of Saint Louis.

Then she, in her turn, entered on this path of heroism,
full of patience and of resignation. Once actually
confined in the Temple, she filled up her time with
tapestry work, and occupied herself with the education
of her children, composing for them a prayer, and
accustoming herself to drink the cup in silence. Her
first chill warning of death was when the head of the
Princess de Lamballe was presented to her at her
prison grating. As she was leaving the Temple to be
transferred to the Conciergerie, she struck her head
against the lintel of the door, having forgotten to stoop ;
and when some one asked if she had hurt herself, 'Oh

no," she replied, "nothing could hurt me now." But
has not each hour of her agony been described? and it
is not our task to tell it over again. I do not believe
it possible that there exists a monument of more
atrocious and ignominious stupidity, than the Procès de
Marie Antoinette, as it is reproduced for any one to
read in vol. xxix. of the *Histoire parlementaire de la
Revolution française.* Most of the replies made by her
to the accusations, are either cut short or suppressed
entirely ; but, as in all iniquitous trials, the text of the
imputations itself bears witness against the murderers.
When we consider that a century, said to be enlightened
and highly cultivated, lent itself to public acts of such
barbarity, we begin to mistrust human nature, and to
feel appalled at its brute ferocity, savage and fierce in
reality, though kept within bounds, and only requiring
opportunity to break forth unrestrainedly. Immediately
after her condemnation, when brought back from the
tribunal to the Conciergerie, Marie Antoinette wrote a
letter, dated the 16th October, half-past four in the
morning; it was addressed to Mme. Elizabeth. In
this letter, a fac-simile of which has recently been
published, and the tone of which breathes the greatest
simplicity, we read: "It is to you, my sister, that I write
for the last time. I have just been condemned, not to a
shameful death, that is only for criminals, but to go and
rejoin your brother. Like him, innocent, I hope to display the same firmness he displayed in his last moments.
I am calm as one is when conscience utters no reproach ;
my one deep regret is to abandon my poor children. You
know that I lived only for them ; and you, my good
and tender sister, you who in your devoted love have
sacrificed everything to be with us, in what a position I
leave you! . . ." The truest sentiments of wife, of friend,
and of a submissive Christian, breathe through this

testamentary letter. We know that Marie Antoinette, a few hours later, gave proof of that calmness and firmness which she hoped to possess at the last moment, and the official report of her executioners acknowledges that she mounted the scaffold with *sufficient courage.*

I do not believe that we are yet in possession of all the elements necessary to enable us to write with fitting simplicity the life of Marie Antoinette ; there exists a collection of her manuscript letters to her brother, the Emperor Joseph, and to the Emperor Leopold, and among the State papers at Vienna there must be a store of such treasures. But I venture to predict, that when these confidential communications see the light of day, they will only confirm the idea which careful reflection and attentive reading of her Memoirs can give us now. The noble mother of Marie Antoinette, from whom she inherited her eagle nose and her queenly bearing, stamped her with the *cachet* of her race ; but the imperial nature, which showed itself only at critical moments, was not her usual disposition, nor the product of her education, nor the spirit of her dreams. She was a daughter of the Cæsars only in emergencies. She was constituted to be the peaceful, pastoral heiress of an empire, rather than to reconquer for herself a kingdom ; before all, beneath her august dignity, she was constituted to be a kind woman, a constant, faithful friend, a tender, devoted mother. She possessed every virtue, every grace, and some of the weaknesses of a woman. Adversity drew out her virtues ; the high-souled dignity of her character revealed itself with more striking pathos because her natural disposition was not so elevated as, through circumstances, it became. Such as she is, the victim of the most hateful, the most brutal sacrifice, an example of the most deplorable vicissitudes, it needs but a little survival of veneration for the old race, to excite a feeling of sympathy and of delicate pity in the breast of every one who reads the story of her brilliant years, and of her later anguish. Every man whose breast contains a spark of the generosity of a Barnave, will be as deeply impressed; and, if it must be said, will be as completely transformed, as he was, when they study closely this noble, outraged woman. As to women, Mme. de Staël long ago put this subject before them, in the way best calculated to touch their hearts, when she said in her *Défense de Marie Antoinette*, "I appeal to you women, who are each and all of you sacrificed in this most tender mother, sacrificed by this outrage perpetrated on weakness; your empire ceases when ferocity triumphs."

Marie Antoinette is more a mother than a queen. We know the prompt reply she made when, being then Dauphiness, and as yet childless, some one in her presence censured a woman who, to obtain the pardon of her son, compromised in a duel, appealed to Mme. du Barry herself: "In her place I would have done the same; and if that had failed, I would have thrown myself at Zamora's feet" (Mme. Du Barry's little negro) "to save my son." And we also remember the last words Marie Antoinette uttered, before that atrocious tribunal, when questioned on shameful imputations regarding the innocence of her son, her sole response was the exclamation, "I appeal to every mother!" This last cry rises above all her life, it is the cry which makes us yearn over her, and which will re-echo through all future time.

One day, at the Temple, an escape was planned, and she had even given her consent. But next day she wrote that she was unable to consent, since flight would necessitate separation from her son. "However great the happiness it would be to me to be far from here, I could not consent to separate from him ... I could find pleasure in nothing if I left my children, and I do not even regret that I cannot go." This, some one will doubtless say, is a very simple sentiment; and it is exactly for that reason that it is beautiful.

MADAME DE LA FAYETTE.

1836.

In Mme. de Sévigné's time, living near her, and one of her dearest friends, was a woman whose history is very closely blended with that of her amiable friend, —the same whom Boileau has described as "*the woman who in all France possessed most wit, and who wrote best.*" This woman wrote but little, however; in her leisure moments only, for her amusement, and with a degree of careless freedom in which there was nothing approaching style. She so specially disliked letter-writing, that only a very few very short letters of hers remain now; it is through Mme. de Sévigné's letters rather than through her own that we are able to form an opinion of her. But she had in her time a distinct influence,—grave, delicate, solid, and charming,—an influence certainly very considerable, and in its way equal to the best. To deep tenderness of heart and a romantic imagination was united great natural accuracy, or, to quote the words of her talented friend, a *divine raison* which never failed her; it is displayed in her writings as in her life, and serves as a model for our consideration in this century, which provides us with such a medley of good models. In restoring the Hôtel de Rambouillet, it has recently been attempted to demonstrate that Mme. de Maintenon was its accomplished and triumphant inheritrix: an expression of Segrais rather decides the dispute about this succession in favour of Mme. de la Fayette, since all those who were called *précieux* had disappeared. After a rather lengthy portrait of Mme. de Rambouillet, he adds at once: "Mme. de la Fayette learned a great deal from her, but Mme. de la Fayette possessed the most intellectual mind," etc. This accomplished disciple of Mme. de Rambouillet, the constant, unchanging friend of Mme. de Sévigné, and also for some time of Mme. de Maintenon, has her assured date and rank in our literature; for she reformed romance, and, through that *divine raison* which was her characteristic, she directed and fixed that tender style which had been excessive, but which it only required her to handle in order to raise it to public favour in comparison with the taste for gravity which had apparently abolished it.

In that subordinate style in which delicacy and a certain degree of interest are sufficient, although genius (should it chance to be encountered) is not unappreciated; which *l'art poétique* does not mention, but which Prévost, Le Sage, and Jean Jacques have exalted (although in the time of Mme. de la Fayette it was confined, at least in her highest conceptions, to the sad passages of *Bérénice* or *Iphigénie*),—in that style, I repeat, Mme. de la Fayette has done precisely that which her illustrious contemporaries, in more highly esteemed and graver styles, tried to accomplish. *L'Astrée*, in implanting, to speak accurately, romance in France, was soon made the parent of an endless offspring, *Cyrus, Cléopâtre, Polexandre*, and *Clélie*. Boileau checked their increase by his sarcasms, as he also repressed that progeny of epic poems, *Moïse sauvé, Saint Louis*, and *La Pucelle*. Mme. de la Fayette, without seeming to ridicule, and, if we may so express it, supported by, or following in the train of these predecessors whom Segrais and Huet confounded with her and wrongfully included in the same cloud of praise, gave them their most successful death-blow in the *Princesse de Clèves*, and what she did accomplish she certainly did intentionally and with due consideration. She was wont to say that one sentence left out in a work was worth a *louis d'or*, and one word twenty *sous*: this saying is most valuable from her, if we consider the romances in ten volumes it was necessary first of all to peruse. Proportion, propriety, and moderation; simple, inspired methods substituted for great catastrophes and grand expressions, these are the distinct signs of the reform, or, to speak less ambitiously, of the improvement she effected on romance; she is a worthy representative of pure Louis XIV. century in this.

The long unbroken tie which existed between Mme. de la Fayette and M. de la Rochefoucauld made her own life like a romance,—a calm romance, yet always a romance, though not so regular as Mme. de Sévigné's, for she loved only her daughter; and not calculating and scheming like Mme. de Maintenon's, whose sole aim was to marry the king. It is interesting to see this tender heart uniting with bitter, disenchanted reason, which it soothes, a late but faithful love between two earnest souls, the more sensible correcting the misanthropical tendencies of the other,—a delicate sentiment, gentleness and mutual comfort rather than delusion and the fire of passion;—a delicate and rather saddened Mme. de Clèves, in short, beside a M. de Nemours grown old and the author of *Maximes:* just such a life was Mme. de la Fayette's, and it exactly corresponds with her romance. That slight illusiveness which we observe in her, that melancholy *raison* which is the core of her life, has slightly tinted even her romantic ideal, and seems to me to permeate all other romances emanating in any way from her influence, and which may be called her posterity, such as Eugène de Rothelin, Mlle. de Clermont, and Edouard. However deep the tenderness may be which breathes through these beautiful creations, reason is there also, experience has whispered promptingly, and cooled all passion. Beside the loving, yielding heart there is a warning and restraining something. M. de la Rochefoucauld is always at the core.

If Mme. de la Fayette reformed romance in France, chivalrous and sentimental romance, and stamped it with that peculiar tone which up to a certain point reconciles the ideal with the practical, we can also say that she gives us the first and an altogether illustrious example of an enduring attachment rendered sacred and legitimate by its constancy * through days and years till death. Such connections belonged to the morals of the old society, and with that society became extinct, or nearly so ; but they could never have existed till after that society was established and fully constituted, which was not till about this time. *La Princesse de Clèves*, and her attachment to M. de la Rochefoucauld, are the two nearly equal titles Mme. de la Fayette possesses to pathetic or serious celebrity ; they are two points which form landmarks in the literature and society of Louis XIV.

I would, however, have left the pleasure and the fancy of rebuilding that life, so simple in events, to the readers of Mme. de Sévigné, if a little unpublished but very intimate document had not enticed me to make a framework for the picture.

* *Exemplum cana simus uterque coma*, the old Latin poet has said.

The father of Mme. de la Fayette, a major-general and governor of Havre, was, it is said, a good man, and carefully directed his daughter's education. Her mother (*née* de Pena) was from Provence, and counted a troubadour poet among her ancestors. Mlle. Marie-Madeleine Pioche de la Vergne had at an early age read and studied more than most of even the cleverest women of the preceding generation had read in their youth. Mme. de Choisy, for example, had extraordinary natural talent in conversation or in letter-writing, but could not even spell. Mme. de Sévigné and Mme. de la Fayette, younger by six or seven years than her friend, possessed, in addition to her excellent grounding, a perfectly cultured mind. Our direct proof as regards this education is furnished by the raptures of Ménage, who, as we know, generally fell in love with his beautiful pupils: he commemorates, under every form of Latin verse, the beauty, grace, and elegance with which Mme. de la Fayette or Mlle. de la Vergne spoke and wrote. At a later period he introduced to her his friend, the learned Huet, who also became one of her literary advisers. Segrais, who shares with Mme. de Sévigné the honour of making Mme. de la Fayette known, tells us: "Three months after Mme. de la Fayette began to learn Latin, she knew more of that language than M.-Ménage or Père Rapin, her tutors. In expounding it to her, they had a dispute concerning the meaning of a passage, and when neither would agree to the rendering of his friend, Mme. de la Fayette said to them, 'You do not either of you understand at all;' and, in fact, she gave them the proper meaning of the passage: they were at once satisfied that she was right. It was one of the poets she expounded, for she was not fond of prose, and had not read Cicero, but, having a great love for poetry, she chiefly read Virgil and Horace; therefore, having the poetic spirit, and understanding the exigencies of the art, she had little trouble in penetrating the meaning of these authors." Further on he alludes to the merits of M. Ménage: "Where shall we find poets like M. Ménage, who wrote good Latin, Greek, and Italian poetry? He was an eminent man, let those who were envious of him say what they like: he did not, however, understand all the delicate shades of meaning in poetry; but Mme. de la Fayette understood them well." This woman, who so highly esteemed and so thoroughly understood the poets, was also so pre-eminently *true*, that M. de la Rochefoucauld, later on, told her so, employing for the first time that expression *vraie*, which is still used: a poetic mind, a true mind, her distinction, like her charm, lies in this union. At the same time, Mme. de la Fayette was most careful (Segrais is again our informant as to this) not to allow anything of her knowledge of Latin to be apparent, so that other women might not be offended. Ménage tells us that she one day replied to M. Huyghens, who asked her what an iambus was, that it was the opposite of a trochee; but it is very certain that it required M. Huyghens and his question to induce her to speak at all on such a subject as an iambus or a trochee.*

She lost her father when she was fifteen. Her

* Tallemant des Reaux, the common reporter of mischievous speeches, attributes one of them to Mlle. de la Vergne on the subject of Ménage, her master: "This most officious Ménage is coming presently." He repeats the story to the end for the sake of showing that the pedantic gallant was not the first thought of all his fair pupils. There is no need of this testimony to prove to us that Mme. de la Fayette was not blind to the defects of the poor Ménage; I even suspect that she thought of him and his platitudes when she remarked that "it was rare to find probity among learned men."

mother, Retz tells us, was a good woman, but rather vain, eager, and bustling. She married again, very soon, the Chevalier Renaud de Sévigné, so much mixed up with the intrigues of the Fronde, and who displayed such zealous activity in aiding the escape of the Cardinal from the Château of Nantes.

In the Memoirs of the Cardinal, we read, *apropos* of this prison of Nantes (1653), and of the entertaining visits he received there: "Mme. de la Vergne, whose second husband was M. le Chevalier de Sévigné, and who lived in Anjou with her husband, came to see me there, and brought with her her daughter, Mlle. de la Vergne, who is now Mme. de la Fayette. She was very pretty and very amiable; and, moreover, had a great resemblance to Mme. de Lesdiguières. She pleased me very much; but, to tell the truth, I did not please her at all, either because she simply did not like me, or it might have been that her mother and step-father, before leaving Paris, had imbued her with a distrust of me, by telling her of my fickleness and inconstancy, and so had prejudiced her against me. I consoled myself for her cruelty with that facility which was so natural to me." Mlle. de la Vergne, at twenty, had need of nothing but her own good sense to teach her to pay no attention to the adventurous prisoner and his idle, quickly-overcome caprice.

Married in 1655 to the Comte de la Fayette, probably the most remarkable and also the most romantic thing about her marriage was that she thus became the sister-in-law of La Mère Angélique de la Fayette, the superior of the Convent of Chaillot, and formerly maid of honour to Anne of Austria, and whose platonic love for Louis XIII. forms a simple chaste romance, very much like those represented in Mme. de Clèves. Her husband having bestowed upon her the name she was destined to render famous, and on which a tender halo already hung, disappears from her life, is blotted out, so to speak; nothing more is heard of him worthy of remark.* She bore her husband two sons, of whom she was very fond,—one a soldier, whose establishment in his profession caused her much anxiety, and who died a short time after her; and the other, the Abbé de la Fayette, who held many good livings, and of whom the chief thing we know is, that he carelessly lent his mother's manuscripts to some one, and lost them.

When very young, Mme. de la Fayette was introduced to the Hôtel de Rambouillet, where she learned a great deal from the Marquise. M. Rœderer, in order to make sure that Molière's witticisms should not affect the Hôtel de Rambouillet, makes out that that distinguished salon had dispersed rather earlier than is quite correct. Mme. de la Fayette had been there even before her marriage, much to her advantage; and also Mme. de Sévigné. M. Auger, in the article he has written on Mme. de la Fayette, which, although otherwise exact and interesting, is dry and stiff, says in regard to this: "Received when very young in the salon of the Hôtel de Rambouillet, her naturally correct and sound judgment might not perhaps have resisted the contagion of the bad taste of which that Hôtel was the centre, if the study of the Latin poets had not acted as an antidote," etc. The antidote had surely acted on Ménage first. All this is most unjust towards the Hôtel de Rambouillet, and M. Rœderer is quite justified in guarding against such criticisms; but he himself

---

* "There is a certain lady who seems to have buried her husband, or at least extinguished him, for there is never any mention made of him in society; no one knows if he is alive or dead."—LA BRUYÈRE.

certainly labours under some misunderstanding if he
makes that Hôtel the cradle of good taste, and yet tells
us that Mlle. de Scudéry was tolerated there instead
of being enthusiastically admired. He forgets that
Voiture, for as long as he lived, engrossed attention
there ; now we know what in regard to wit Voiture
was, but we also know what he was in regard to taste.
As for Mlle. de Scudéry, we have only to read Segrais,
Huet, and others, to see how they esteem that incomparable young authoress and her illustrious *Bassa* and
the *Grand Cyrus*, and her poetry, so tender and so natural,
which Despréaux so maliciously attacked and yet was
unable to rival ; and surely that which Segrais and
Huet both equally admired ought not to be more
severely criticised by a circle of which they were the
oracles. Mme. de la Fayette, with her sound sense
and keen understanding, gleaned, like Mme. de Sévigné,
the best from intellectual intercourse. Her youth
brought her into close connection with the young court
circle, and even had her mind been less sensible, she
could not have failed to acquire a correct and courtly
elegance. Since the beginning of her married life, she
had been accustomed to see frequently at the Convent
of Chaillot, the young princess of England, with Queen
Henrietta, who, during her exile, had retired there.
When the young princess became *Madame*, and the
brightest ornament of the court, Mme. de la Fayette,
although ten years her senior, kept up her old intimacy
with her, had constant private intercourse with her,
and was considered her favourite. In the charming
account she has written of some of the brilliant years
of this princess's life, speaking of herself in the third
person, she thus criticises herself : " Mlle. de la Tremouille and Mme. de la Fayette were of this number
(*the number of persons who saw Madame frequently*). The

first-named was agreeable to *Madame* on account of her goodness, and a certain ingenuous habit she had of telling her inmost thoughts, which took one back to the simplicity of an earlier age ; the other pleased her by some good fortune ; for, although she possessed some merit, it was of such a serious kind that it seemed unlikely to be pleasing to a princess as young as *Madame*." Thus, when she was about thirty years of age, Mme. de la Fayette found herself in the very centre of that fashion and gaiety which reigned during the most flourishing years of Louis XIV.'s time ; she was a guest at all *Madame's* entertainments at Fontainebleau or at St. Cloud, but a spectator rather than one who took an active part, as she herself truthfully tells us when relating certain things, although after the things had happened and began to be talked about, the princess told her about them and made her write them down. " You write well," *Madame* said to her ; " write, and I shall furnish you with some amusing memoirs." "This was a difficult enough task," confesses Mme. de la Fayette, "for in certain places I had to disguise the truth in such a way that it would still be recognisable, and yet not offend or displease the princess." One of the passages which required all Mme. de la Fayette's most delicate tact, and which provoked the amused wit of *Madame* at the trouble the amiable scribe gave herself, must, I should imagine, have been this: " She (*Madame*) is intimate with the Comtesse de Soissons, . . . and now only thinks of pleasing the King as his sister-in-law. I am sure she pleases him in quite another way, and I am sure also that she thinks he only pleases her as a brother-in-law, although he probably pleases her more ; but, to sum up, as they are both infinitely agreeable, and are both endowed by nature with amorous dispositions, and as they see each other every day in a world of pleasure and amusement, it appears to all the world that they entertain for each other that liking which usually precedes a *grande passion.*"

Madame died in Mme. de la Fayette's arms, who, at the last, never left her bedside for a moment. The story she tells of that death equals the most beautiful account we ever read of the most pathetic death; it runs in the following simple words, which illuminate the scene: "I went up to her room. She told me she was fretful, and the peevishness with which she spoke would have sounded beautifully amiable from another woman, so much natural sweetness did she possess, and so little was she capable of petulant temper. . . . After dinner, she lay down on the floor, and made me sit beside her in such a way that her head half rested on me. During her sleep she changed so much, that, after looking at her a long time, I began to be surprised, and I thought how greatly expression beautified her face. . . . I was wrong, however, to make such a reflection, for I had often seen her asleep, yet never less lovely." And again: "*Monsieur* was by her bedside; she kissed him, saying sweetly, and in a tone which might have melted the hardest heart, 'Alas! *Sir*, you left off loving me a long time ago; but this was unjust: I never failed in my duty towards you.' *Monsieur* appeared to be deeply moved, and all who were in the room were so much affected that nothing was heard but the sound of weeping. . . . When the King had left her room, I was by her bedside; she said to me, 'Mme. de la Fayette, my nose is already sunken.' I could only answer by my tears; and she sank very fast." On the 30th June 1673, Mme. de la Fayette wrote to Mme. de Sévigné: "It is three years to-day since I saw *Madame* die: yesterday, I read over many of her letters; my thoughts are full of her."

In the midst of this gay and social circle, still young, and with a face which, if not beautiful, was pleasant and aristocratic, was Mme. de la Fayette for ten years but an attentive observer, with no active personal interest other than her attachment to *Madame*, had she no peculiar secret preference of her own? About the year 1665, as I suppose, and as I shall explain further on, she had chosen outside this whirl of gaiety her own peculiar friend, M. de la Rochefoucauld, at that time fifty-two.

She began to write early from a natural inclination, but even then with earnest sense. Portraits were then in vogue. About 1659, Mme. de la Fayette wrote one of Mme. de Sévigné, which is reputed to have been the work of an unknown author. "It flatters me," said the latter, on finding it among some old dusty papers of Mme. de la Tremouille's in 1675, "but those who loved me sixteen years ago would have found some resemblance in it." It is these youthful features which her friend has fixed for all time, which come before our mind's eye when we think of the immortal Mme. de Sévigné. When *Madame* persuaded Mme. de la Fayette to write for her, saying to her, "*You write well,*" she had, no doubt, read *La Princesse de Montpensier*, our author's first short novel, which was published in 1660 or 1662.*
In elegance and vivacity of style it is distinctly superior to the other novels and stories of the time, and introduces a spirit of justice and reform. In composition, Mme. de la Fayette's imagination was readily carried back to the brilliant and polished epoch of the Valois,

* *Le Dictionnaire de Moréri* says 1662, and *Quérard* 1660. But it is quite certain that the first edition published with the King's permission was in 1662, and without any author's name.

to the reigns of Charles IX. or Henri II., which she idealized a little, or embellished after the manner of those graceful and tactfully discreet tales in which Queen Marguerite pourtrays them for us. *La Princesse de Montpensier*, *La Princesse de Clèves*, *La Comtesse de Tende*, are all within those reigns, the vices and the crimes of which have perhaps too vividly eclipsed in our eyes their brilliant intellectual culture. As regards wit or intellect, intrigue, and also vice, the court of *Madame* was not without its resemblance to the courts of the Valois, and the history of it which Mme. de la Fayette has written, recalls more than once the Mémoires of the queen, so charming in her time, but whom we must not therefore always believe. The perfidious Vardes and the proud M. de Guiche are in reality characters who would be quite in keeping with the court of Henri II.; and in that court of *Madame's*, a Chevalier de Lorraine was not wanting. Mme. de la Fayette had an influence of some weight in this society, and exercised a wise criticism on its tone. Two months before the unfortunate death of *Madame*, Mme. de Montmorency wrote to M. de Bussy by way of jest (1st May 1670): " Mme. de la Fayette, *Madame's* favourite, has broken her head against the cornice of the chimney-piece, which had no respect for a head brilliant with the glory lent to it by the favour of so great a princess. Before this misfortune a letter of hers appeared, which she made public, to ridicule what are called fashionable words, the use of which is unnecessary; I send it to you." Then follows the letter, which is entirely composed of the nonsensical jargon used in the fashionable world, and which she wished to correct. The letter is from a jealous lover to his mistress. Boileau could not have surpassed it in style. Mme. de la Fayette, although a degree softer, was the Despréaux (Boileau) of courtly language.

In the end of this same year, 1670, *Zayde* appeared. It was Mme. de la Fayette's first real work, for *La Princesse de Montpensier* was not a serious effort, and had not been noticed at the time except by a very few people. *Zayde* was published in Segrais' name, and was something more than a purely transparent fiction. The public readily believed that Segrais was the author. Bussy received the book as the work of Segrais, and anticipated much pleasure from its perusal; "for Segrais," he remarked, "could not write what is not good." After reading it, he criticised and praised it, still in the same belief. Since that time many persons have maintained that to Segrais the honour of its creation belongs, or at all events that a great deal of it was written by him. Adry, who in 1807 published an edition of *La Princesse de Clèves*, in leaving the question rather vague and doubtful, seems inclined to favour the idea that it was the production of the talented poet.

But the worthy Adry, who is an authority as a bibliographer, has a rather slavishly literal mind. Segrais, however, tells us quite plainly, it seems to me, in the conversations and sayings of his which have been collected: "*La Princesse de Clèves* is by Mme. de la Fayette. . . . *Zayde*, which appeared in my name, is also hers. It is true I had collaborated, but only as regards the arrangement of the romance, in which the rules of art are observed with great exactitude." It is, moreover, true that at another time Segrais said: "After my *Zayde* was published, Mme. de la Fayette ordered one copy to be bound with white paper between each page, so that she might revise and correct it, particularly the language; but she found nothing in it to correct, even years after, and I do not suppose any one could improve it even at this date." It is evident that Segrais, like so many quite honest editors, allowed himself to slip into the phrase *my Zayde*, yet blushed a little when others spoke of it as his. This confusion of author and editor is simple and natural enough. In the middle ages, and even in the sixteenth century, a Latin phrase copied or quoted was as much a matter of pride to an author as an original idea, and if he should be the first to call attention to a romance or a romance writer, he is even more touchy on the subject: such foster-parents do not dislike the soft impeachment, and only half refute it. But without this, through constantly hearing their own name in connection with the praise or criticism of the work, they cling all the more closely to their adoption. If I remember rightly, people used so constantly to identify me with *Ronsard*, that I had difficulty in keeping from saying *my Ronsard*. One feels flattered also to have been the first to patronise a good novel, or even a bad one. The worthy Adry, then, far from having any malicious intention, adopts without sufficient proof this expression of Segrais, *my Zayde*. Huet is explicit enough on the subject in his *Origines de Caën*; he is still more so in his Latin *Commentaire* on himself. "Ill-informed people," he says, "regard it as an insult that I should have chosen to speak of Segrais as I did in *Les Origines de Caën;* but I can certify the fact on the testimony of my own eyes and from a number of Mme. de la Fayette's own letters; for she sent me each part of the work as fast as she composed it, and made me read and revise it." Lastly, Mme. de la Fayette often said to Huet, who had bound up along with *Zayde* his treatise on the *Origine des Romans:* "Do you know that we have married our children?"

Certainly, after all, the style of *Zayde* is not so notably different from the style of Segrais' novels but that at the time people might have mistaken them. *Zayde* still belongs to the pure old romantic style, although it is a gem of its kind; and if the reform has already commenced there, it is solely in the detail, in the way the story is told rather than in the actual conception itself. *Zayde*, to some extent, may be said to hold a middle place between *L'Astrée* and the romances of the Abbé Prevost, and is a connecting link between them. We find the same sudden and extraordinary passions, unheard-of resemblances, prolonged adventures and mistakes, resolutions made at sight of a portrait or a bracelet. Unhappy lovers quit the court and all its pleasures for dreary deserts, where, however, all their wants are supplied; they pass the afternoons in woods, and recite their miseries to the rocks, and when they re-enter their homes they find all kinds of beautiful pictures there. By chance they encounter on the seashore unfortunate princesses lying apparently lifeless, having escaped shipwreck in magnificent attire, and who languidly open their eyes only to fall in love with them. Shipwrecks, deserts, arrivals, and ecstasies; therefore, still the old romance of Héliodore or of Urfé, the romantic Spanish style of Cervantes' novels. The peculiarity of Mme. de la Fayette is her extremely delicate analysis; the most tender sentiments are unravelled by her with the utmost subtlety. The jealousy of Alphonse, which appeared so unlikely to her contemporaries, and which Segrais tells us was taken from real life, and rather lessened than exaggerated, is depicted with vivid skill both in the early and later stages of his trouble. Here the excellence of the work makes itself felt, there observation is displayed. A fine passage, and one which has been qualified as admirable by D'Alembert, is where the two lovers, who had been separated less than two months before, neither knowing the other's language, meet again, each speaking in the language of the other,

which they have learned in the interval : then suddenly
they stop short, blushing as at a mutual confession.
For my own part, I prefer some sentimental remarks
like this, which Mme. de la Fayette certainly did not
write without some secret reference to her own feelings :
"Ah ! Don Garcia, you are right : there are no passions
except those which seize us at once, take us by surprise;
the others are merely intimacies our hearts are volun-
tarily drawn into. True attachments draw us in spite
of ourselves."

Mme. de la Fayette did not, I think, understand
these passions which fight to overmaster us ; she gave
her heart willingly, impulsively. When her heart's
affections became fixed on M. de la Rochefoucauld,
she must have been, as I have said, about thirty-two or
thirty-three, and he fifty-two. She had doubtless been
acquainted with him for some time, but it is of their
peculiar connection that I mean to speak. We shall
see by the following letter, now published for the first
time, and which is one of the most confidential letters
we could desire, that about the time the *Maximes* were
published, and just at the time when the Comte de
Saint-Paul first began to go into society, there was a
rumour of this connection between Mme. de la Fayette
and M. de la Rochefoucauld as of an intimacy very
recently established. Now, the publication of the
Maximes and the Comte de Saint-Paul's appearance in
society, allowing him to have been sixteen or seventeen,
exactly coincide, and make the date 1665 or 1666.
Mme. de la Fayette wrote the letter to Mme. de Sablé,
an old friend of M. de la Rochefoucauld's, and one whose
influence considerably affected the composition of the
Maximes, and who had been for some time a devoted
disciple of Port-Royal, rather through fear of death finding her still unreformed than from any sincere feeling of

conversion. "Monday Evening," the letter is dated. " I
was unable to reply to your letter yesterday because
I had company, and I fear I shall not be able to reply to
it to-day because I find it too flattering. I am ashamed
of the praise you bestow on me, but on the other hand
I like you to have a good opinion of me, and I have no
wish to contradict your idea of me. Therefore, in
replying to you, I shall only say that the Comte de
Saint-Paul has just gone, and that we have spoken
about you for a whole hour, and you can imagine how
I would speak on such a subject. We also discussed
a man whom I always take the liberty of comparing
with you in intellectual charm. I do not know if the
comparison offend you, but if it should offend you
from another's lips, it is great praise from mine, if all
we hear be true. I soon saw that the Comte de Saint-
Paul had heard these things which are said, and I went
into the matter slightly with him. But I am afraid he
did not take what I said seriously. I beg of you, the first
time you see him, to speak to him of these rumours. This
will come quite naturally, for I have given him the
Maximes, and he will tell you so, no doubt. But I
implore you to speak to him of them most certainly, to
give him the idea that the matter is nothing but a joke.
I am not sufficiently aware of your own opinion to be
sure that you will say the right thing; and I think it
might be best to begin by convincing the ambassador.
I must trust the matter to your skill, however; it is
superior to ordinary maxims; only convince him. I
have a horror that persons of his age should imagine
that I am frivolous or a coquette. They seem to think
everybody older than themselves a hundred, and are
quite astonished they should still be considered interesting; moreover, he would more readily believe what
was said to him of M. de la Rochefoucauld than of

another. So I do not wish him to think anything
about it, except that he is one of my friends, and I pray
that you will not forget to drive this out of his head if
it is in it, any more than I have forgotten your message.
It is not very generous, however, to remind you of a
service when asking you to do me one." In a postscript
she adds: "I must not forget to mention that I found
the Comte de Saint-Paul terribly quick-witted."

To give additional interest to this letter, let us try to
realize the exact situation: M. de Saint-Paul, the son
of Mme. de Longueville, and probably also of M. de la
Rochefoucauld, coming to call on Mme. de la Fayette,
who is said to be the object of a late and tender passion,
but who would like to undeceive him—or to deceive
him, rather. The *terrible quick-wittedness* of the young
man went straight, I expect, to Mme. de Longueville's
heart; no doubt, she was soon shown the postscript, if
not the whole of the letter. The most charming part
of the letter, and which all elderly lovers ought to
inwardly digest, "I have a horror of persons of his age
thinking me capable of coquetry," exactly responds to
this passage in the *Princesse de Clèves:* "Mme. de Clèves,
who was at the age at which it is impossible to believe
that a woman who is over twenty-five can be loved,
regarded with extreme surprise the king's attachment
to this duchess (de Valentinois)." The idea was Mme.
de la Fayette's own, we see. She specially dreaded
appearing either to inspire or to feel love at an age
when others seek it. Her delicate sense became her
last effort of modesty.

I am more firm in my conviction that the peculiar
and well-known *liaison* between M. de la Rochefoucauld
and her only began about this time, because it seems
to me so apparent that this affectionate friend's influence
over him was expressly contrary to the *Maximes;* that

had she been near him before they were written, as she was afterwards, she would have made him correct and simplify them; and that La Rochefoucauld, the misanthrope, he who said he had never found love except in romances, and that for his own part he had never experienced it, is not the same man almost, of whom she said at a later period, "M. de la Rochefoucauld has taught me wisdom, but I have reformed his heart."

In a short (unpublished) note from her to Mme. de Sablé, who had herself composed *Maximes*, I read : " It will disappoint me more than I can express if you do not show me your *Maximes*. Mme. du Plessis has inspired me with an extraordinary desire to see them, and it is simply because they are honest and sensible that I have this desire, and because they will convince me that all sensible persons are not so certain about universal depravity as M. de la Rochefoucauld is." It is this idea of universal depravity which she sets herself to overcome in M. de la Rochefoucauld, and which she reforms. The wish to soften and brighten this noble mind was doubtless a kind-hearted and reasonable excuse for her at the beginning of their close intimacy.

The old chevalier of the Fronde, grown bitter and gouty, was, besides, not exactly the kind of man his book alone would lead us to suppose he was. He had studied little, Segrais tells us, but his marvellous sense and his knowledge of the world supplied the place of studious learning. In his youth he had plunged into all the vices of his time, and withdrew with a mind more healthy than his body, if we can call such a cynical mind healthy. His cynicism in no way detracted from the fascinating charm of his society. He was courtesy personified always, and improved on close acquaintance. Delightful in close and intimate conversation, his low-toned voice just suited him. If he had been obliged to solemnly address five or six persons, his voice would have lacked strength ; and the customary oration at the Academy Française deterred him from seeking admission there. In June 1672, when in one evening the death of Mme. de Longueville, that of the Chevalier de Marsallac, his grandson, and the wound of his son, the Prince de Marsallac,—when his *hailstorm* of misfortune fell upon him,—Mme. de Sévigné tells us, his grief and his self-control were admirable. "I saw his heart bared," she adds, "in that cruel time ; I never have beheld such courage, goodness, tenderness, and sense." A short time later, she said of him that his nature was domesticated, and that he understood almost as well as she did, maternal love. This is the real De la Rochefoucauld, such as he became under Mme. de la Fayette's reforming influence.

From 1666 to 1670, Mme. de la Fayette (who was not so delicate as she afterwards became), through the favour in which *Madame* held her, had occasion and opportunity of going very frequently to court: it was not till just after the death of *Madame*, and also about the time her health began to fail, that the *liaison*, as Mme. de Sévigné points out, became an established fact. The letters of the *incomparable* friend, which are written with uninterrupted regularity from this very time, give us insight into the most trifling circumstances, and even allow us to enter into the pleasant monotony of that deeply tender companionship. "Their delicate health," she writes, "makes them necessary to each other, and . . . gives them leisure to enjoy each other's good qualities, to a degree which is unusual in such circumstances. . . . At court there is no leisure time for loving : that vortex, so violent for others, was tranquil to them, and left plenty of time for their delightful intercourse. My opinion is, that no passion could be stronger than such a bond." I do not quote all it would be possible to extract from each letter of Mme. de Sévigné's in the same strain ; for there are very few in which Mme. de la Fayette is not mentioned, and several of them are written from her house with messages enclosed from M. de la Rochefoucauld himself. On good days, days of tolerable health and of dinners *en bavardinage*, as she expresses it, there is a charming playfulness, trills of amusing scandal on the eccentricities of Mme. de Marans, the domestic arrangements of Mme. de Brissac and M. le Duc. Then there are quieter but not less delightful days, when at Saint-Maur, in the house which M. le Prince had lent to Gourville, and of which Mme. de la Fayette had free use, they listened in a select company to the poetry of Despréaux, which was considered a *chef-d'œuvre*. On another day, despising Despréaux and his poetry, they went to hear Lulli, and would shed tears at certain passages in the opera of *Cadmus*. "I was not the only one who could not listen unmoved," said Mme. de Sévigné ; "the soul of Mme. de la Fayette was also deeply troubled." Is not that *troubled soul* tenderness itself! Oh, *Zayde, Zayde!* we perceive in the trouble of your heart that tender romance which is but half satisfied, and which will not bear to be too deeply stirred. There are also days on which Mme. de la Fayette still goes to court, not formally, but to pay a little visit, and the king makes her sit in his barouche with the ladies-in-waiting, and points out to her all the beauties of Versailles, as any private gentleman might do; and such visits, and such attentions, wise and modest as she is, furnish on her return food for long conversations, and even for letters not quite so short as usual from Mme. de la Fayette, who is not fond of letter-writing; and Mme. de Grignan, far away, is rather jealous, and becomes still more so about some little writing-table made of wood from Saint-Lucie, which Mme. de Montespan had presented to Mme. de la Fayette;* but Mme. de Sévigné puts this all right again by the compliments she is continually exchanging between her daughter and her best friend. Even when Mme. de la Fayette no longer went to Versailles, no longer with tears of gratitude embraced the king's knees, even when M. de la Rochefoucauld was dead, she preserved her respect and consideration. Mme. de Sévigné tells us that "no woman ever managed her affairs so well without loss of dignity." Louis XIV. always liked her because she had been *Madame's* favourite; he always remembered that she was a witness of that sad death, and also of those happy years with which she would for ever be associated, for she had seldom appeared at court since.

But Versailles, and *La poétique* of Despréaux,† and the opera of Lulli, and all the fun over Mme. de Marans, are constantly interrupted by that miserable health, which, with its accompanying low fever, could not be

---

* We gather from Mme. de Sévigné's letters that Mme. de Grignan must frequently have said, "As for your Mme. de la Fayette, does she love you so marvellously well? She scarcely writes two lines to you in ten years; she knows how to do what suits her best; she takes things easily; but, in the midst of her indolence, she has an eye to her own interests." Gourville, with whom unfortunately Mme. de la Fayette was for a long time very frank and unreserved as with a faithful friend, has written something of the same kind about her, or more malicious still. Lassay, in some *Mémoires* he has published, also insinuates against Mme. de la Fayette that she looked after her own interests, and knew how to take advantage; but one must hear both sides before making up one's mind.

† Boileau.—Tr.

ignored, and gradually became her chief concern. In her large and beautiful garden in *La Rue de Vaugirard*, so green and perfumed; in Gourville's house at Saint-Maur, where she was quite at home; at Fleury-sous-Meudon, where she went to breathe the woodland air, we follow her, ill and sad; we see that long, melancholy face getting thin and pinched. Her life for twenty years is but a slowly consuming fever, and the bulletins always come to this: "Mme. de la Fayette leaves to-morrow for a small house opposite Meudon, where she has been before. She will spend a fortnight there, lingering as it were between heaven and earth; with no desire to think or speak, or to listen or reply; it tires her to say good-morning or good-evening; she is so feverish every day that repose is the only remedy, therefore she must have repose. I shall go and see her sometimes. M. de la Rochefoucauld is resting on that couch which you remember; he is miserably depressed, and it is easy to see what is the cause." The cause was certainly a worse misfortune than gout or any of his ordinary troubles,—it was the absence of Mme. de la Fayette.

The melancholy depression which such a condition naturally induced did not prevent the charm and the smile reappearing at short intervals. In the nicknames then in vogue, which made of Mme. Scarron *The Thaw*, of Colbert *The North*, of M. de Pomponne *Rain*, Mme. de la Fayette was called *The Mist:* the mist cleared off at times, and then the most charming horizons appeared. A sweet, resigned, and melancholy nature, interesting and engaging; a composed voice, sowing good and impressive words, formed the constant attraction of her conversation and ideas. "*It is sufficient to love*," she would say, accepting her condition of inactivity. This expression, which exactly describes her, is worthy of her who also said, *à propos* of Montaigne, that it would be a pleasure to have a neighbour like him.

At times this calmness would suddenly be moved to tears, like a spring gushing forth from smooth ground; stirred to the depths of her sensitive nature, as we have seen her moved by the power of music. When Mme. de Sévigné was going to the Rochers or to Provence, and went to say good-bye, one might have supposed that visit was to be her last: Mme. de la Fayette's tender heart could not bear unmoved the departure of such a friend. One day, M. le Duc being present, some one spoke of the campaign which was to begin in six months; the sudden realization of the dangers M. le Duc would be exposed to at once drew forth tears. This emotion was both flattering and charming, we may imagine, in one usually so calm and sensible.

In the midst of all her weakness, she did not neglect essential matters; unable to move, she yet attended to everything. If she reformed the heart of M. de la Rochefoucauld, she also rectified his affairs. She got his lawsuit satisfactorily arranged, and prevented him losing the best of his estates by providing him with the means of proving that they were entailed. Still, it is understood, she wrote few letters, and only necessary ones. This was her only ground of dispute with Mme. de Sévigné. Of the few letters of hers which remain, nearly all are to say that she merely writes two lines, that she would write more had she not a headache; and one day, M. de la Fayette, who conveniently and unexpectedly arrives from I know not where, is turned into an excuse. We have but to read the charming letter, "*Well! well! my dear, what is the matter that you scream like an eagle?*" etc., to thoroughly apprehend the measure of Mme. de la Fayette's life, and to understand the difference between her style and Mme. de Sévigné's. In that letter we read the words, so often quoted: "You are in Provence, my dear; your hours are free, and your head more so; you like to write to everybody, my taste for writing to everybody is gone, and if I had a lover who required a letter from me every morning, I would break with him."

Mme. de la Fayette was very sincere and very frank; *one was impelled to trust her word.** She would pay no honour or respect unless where she was satisfied it was due; and on this account she has been called severe, whilst she was but discriminating.† Mme. de Maintenon, with whom Mme. de la Fayette had much in common, possessed also a very just mind, but her nature was not so frank; judicious also, but less sincere; and these dissimilarities, no doubt, helped to cool their friendship. In 1672, when Mme. Scarron was secretly bringing up the illegitimate children of Loüis XIV. in a secluded part of the Faubourg Saint-Germain, near Vaugirard, some distance beyond Mme. de la Fayette's house, the former was still very friendly with her; she often enjoyed a chat with her, and also with Mme. de Coulanges; they must even have visited together. But Mme. Scarron's intimacy gradually became less confidential, the result being that tales were repeated, and conjectures were made, which caused unpleasantness between the friends. "The idea of a religious life never entered my mind," wrote Mme. de Maintenon to the Abbé Testu; "therefore you may reassure Mme. de la Fayette." Giving her brother some hints on economy Mme. de Maintenon wrote in 1678: "Even if I had fifty thousand *livres*, I should not play the *grande dame*, neither could I have a bed with gold lace hangings

* Mme. de Sévigné. † Segraisiana.

like Mme. de la Fayette, nor a *valet-de-chambre* like Mme. de Coulanges. Is the pleasure derived from such luxuries worth the sarcasms they rouse?" I do not know if Mme. de la Fayette's gold-embroidered bed lent itself well to such witticisms; but lying on it, as too often happened, she was certainly more simple than her friend in that mantle the colour of dead leaves which she affected to the end. At last friendship between them entirely ceased. Mme. de Maintenon made that known: "I have not been able to preserve Mme. de la Fayette's friendship, she exacted too much for its continuance. I have at least shown her that I am as sincere as she is. The Duke is the cause of our misunderstanding. We have before misunderstood each other in small matters."* And in Mme. de la Fayette's Mémoires we find, under the years 1688 and 1689, *à propos* of the *Comedie d'Esther:* "She" (Mme. de Maintenon) "commanded a poet to write a comedy, but to choose a pious subject, for at present there is no safety for the court either here or in another world except in piety. . . . The comedy illustrates in some way the fall of Mme. de Montespan and the elevation of Mme. de Maintenon; the only difference being that Esther was a little younger and less affected in her piety." In quoting the words of these two illustrious women, it gives me no pleasure to rake up again the bitterness which destroyed a long friendship. The fact is, Mme. de Maintenon and Mme. de la Fayette

---

* Letter to Mme. de Saint Géran, August 1684. Of what Duke does she speak? Is it the new Duc de la Rochefoucauld? We see from one of Mme. de Maintenon's letters to the same lady (April 1679) that she could not endure the Marsallacs, father and son. All these letters to Mme. de Saint Géran have become very untrustworthy since the last criticisms on La Beaumelle's edition.

were both important and influential women, and they
took too little trouble to retain each other's regard.
Mme. de Maintenon's elevation being the latest, she
no doubt gradually changed towards Mme. de la
Fayette, who remained the same as before ; it was this
very consistency of conduct which was irritating to
Mme. de Maintenon, who probably would have liked to
see her change a little with her fortune. Mme. de la
Fayette ill and dying was still the same as when Mme.
Scarron, writing to Mme. de Chantelou on her present-
ation to Mme. de Montespan in 1666, said of her : "Mme.
de Thianges introduced me to her sister. . . . I made
my distress apparent . . . without putting it into words;
. . . so Mme. de la Fayette would have been pleased
by the sincerity of my expressions, and the brevity with
which they were delivered." Had I been M. Rœderer,
and wished to give an example of amiable and refined
society in which grace mingled with gravity and
sincerity, I should have found it in the circle composed
by Mme. de Sévigné and Mme. de la Fayette, rather
than in Mme. de Maintenon's successful elevation and
marriage. The latter, in a sense, injured refined society,
as certain revolutionaries have injured liberty by push-
ing it too far, and forcing excesses which call forth
reaction in an opposite direction. She should have
avoided extreme prudishness or over strictness, and so
have delayed the excesses of the *Regency*.

In July 1677, a year before the publication of the
Princesse de Clèves, we find that Mme. de la Fayette's
health was at its worst, although she still had fifteen
years to pine and suffer before release came, being *one
of those who drag out their miserable existence to the last
drop of oil.** It was in the following winter, however,
that M. de la Rochefoucauld and she put the final

* Mme. de Sévigné.

touches to the charming romance which was issued by
Barbier on the 16th of March 1678. Segrais, who again
crosses our path, says, in one place, that he has not
taken the trouble to reply to the criticisms which were
made on this romance; and in another place, that
Mme. de la Fayette has not condescended to reply to
them; so that we are free to speculate as to the extent
of his co-operation. But we shall not discuss this at
present, and the romance is too superior to anything he
has ever written to admit of any hesitation. Besides,
no one was deceived: those who read it in confidence had
spoken of it; and the book was well received as the
work of Mme. de la Fayette alone, aided by M. de la
Rochefoucauld's good taste. As soon as this *Princesse*,
so long heralded, appeared, it was the chief topic of
conversation and of correspondence. Bussy and Mme.
de Sévigné wrote to each other about it; everywhere
people were full of curiosity about it, stopping each
other in the broad walk of the Tuileries to exchange
opinions regarding it. Fontenelle read the romance four
times, always finding something new in it; Boursault
composed a tragedy from it, as now it would have been
turned into a vaudeville; Valincour wrote anonymously
a little volume of criticism which was attributed to
Père Bonhours; and an Abbé de Charnes replied by
another little volume, with which Barbier d'Aucourt,
the celebrated critic of the time, and the habitual enemy
of the spiritual Jesuit, was credited. The *Princesse
de Clèves* has survived to obtain the reputation it
deserved, and remains the earliest of our most esteemed
romances.

It is pathetic to think of the peculiar circumstances
in which these pure and charming creations were composed,—these noble, stainless characters, so healthy, so
accomplished, so tender; for Mme. de la Fayette

endows them with all her loving and romantic soul retains of early, ever-cherished dreams. M. de la Rochefoucauld, too, had been delighted to discover in M. de Nemours that brilliant bloom of chivalry which he himself had so abused, a beautiful mirror in which his own youth lives again.* Thus did those two old friends return in imagination to that early time when they neither knew nor loved each other. That well-known blush of Mme. de Clèves, which at first is almost her only language, distinctly marks the author's idea, which is to picture love as all that is freshest and most modest, most agitating, undecided, and irresistible,— most *itself*, in a word. There is a constant study of *that delight which youth and beauty give; of that embarrassed agitation in every act which, in the innocence of early youth, love causes;* in short, she dwells on all which is most unlike herself and her friend, and their tardy affection. In the ordinary things of life she was especially sensible ; her judgment was superior to her wit, it was said of her, and this praise flattered her more than anything: here poetry and sensitiveness are uppermost, though judgment never fails. Nowhere as in the *Princesse de Clèves* have the contradictions and the delicate duplicities of love been so naturally expressed. "Mme. de Clèves had in the beginning been annoyed that M. de Nemours had been led to suppose that she had prevented him going to the Maréchal de Saint-André's house ; then afterwards she was vexed that her mother enlightened him as to the truth. . . . Mme. de Clèves was very much afraid that the prince would discover her partiality for him ; and his words

* The Abbé Longuerne tells us M. de la Rochefoucauld remained all his life faithful to his love of romance. Every afternoon he and Segrais used to meet at Mme. de la Fayette's to read *L'Astrée*. He retained throughout a taste for romance.

showed her that she was not mistaken. She was much
distressed to find that she was no longer able to hide
her feelings, and that she had allowed them to be seen
by the Chevalier de Guise. She was also sorry that M.
de Nemours knew of her feelings; but this last trouble
was not so deep, and it was blended with a certain
degree of sweetness." The action of the plot is always
correct, well concentrated, conversational, unlikely only
in one or two instances, although this is scarcely
discovered on account of the interest one is made to
feel in the story. The episodes are never too lengthy;
they rather help than retard the progress of the plot.
The most unlikely episode, that of the pavilion, when
M. de Nemours arrives in a very remarkable manner,
just in time to hear from behind a palisade the avowal
made to Mme. de Clèves,—this scene, which Bussy and
Valincour pick to pieces, nevertheless, according to
the latter, drew tears from the eyes even of such as would
scarcely be affected by *Iphigénie*. To us who are little
disquieted by unlikely episodes, and who love the
Princesse de Clèves and its rather old-fashioned style,
what charms us most is the want of exaggeration in
those scenes which are so expressive, the ever-present
vein of gentle dreaminess, the lover strolling by the
willow-shaded stream; and the vivid description of
the loved one's beauty, *her hair carelessly caught up;*
again, *her eyes slightly dilated* by tears; and, to give a
last quotation, *that life which was short enough*, the
impression she herself was deeply conscious of. The
language also is charming, delicate, and exquisitely
chosen,* with some careless yet graceful irregularities,

* A critic we are pleased to quote, has said: "It is very
remarkable to observe how, under Louis XIV., the French
language in all its purity, as written by Mme. de la Fayette,
Mme. de Sévigné, and M. de la Rochefoucauld, is composed of a

and which Valincour only specified in case they should be condemned by a grammarian of his acquaintance, but feeling almost ashamed to make them any reproach to the charming authoress.

The little volume by Valincour, which Adry has republished in his edition of the *Princesse de Clèves*, is a distinguished specimen of polite criticism, such as amateurs of taste indulged in under Louis XIV. Valincour was only twenty-five at the time; he did not associate with Huet and Segrais; he belonged to a later generation, and was the issue of Racine's and Boileau's teaching. His malice, which was always temperate, did not prevent him being just, and giving praise where it was due; he has not, however, restrained from captious cavilling over details. Those who attributed the criticism to Père Bonhours, had cause to find it comical that the censor objects to the first meeting of M. de Clèves and Mlle. de Chartres having taken place in a jeweller's shop rather than in a church. However, the whole shows a sharp, discriminating judgment, discreetly sarcastic,—such sarcasm as Fontanes might have consulted with pleasure and profit before criticising Mme. de Staël. The Abbé de Charnes, who replies to this criticism word for word, refutes it with scorn, but, in my opinion, in the style of a provincialist who had not asked Mme. de la Fayette's permission to defend her; Barbier d'Aucourt, without possessing any very delicate powers, would have acquitted himself otherwise. Valincour, it is apparent, has a complete theory about the historical romance, which is so very well exemplified by a scholar whom

few expressions which in conversation constantly recur with a charm of their own. . . . One can say, especially as regards Mme. de la Fayette's style, that it was purity and transparency itself,—the *liquida vox* of Horace."

he brings forward;. this theory is the same as that which Walter Scott has partly realized.

Bussy, who in his letters to Mme. de Sévigné speaks at considerable length of the *Princesse de Clèves*, adds, with that incredible self-conceit which spoils the effect: "Our criticism is the criticism of cultivated people who possess *ésprit*; printed criticism is more pungent and amusing in many instances." To avenge Mme. de la Fayette for some of the malice perpetrated by that presumptuous individual, we need only quote from him the above characteristic remark.

As she progressed with the *Princesse de Clèves*, Mme. de la Fayette, after her first retrospective allusions to youth and its delights, becomes grave again; and duty gradually comes to be her chief thought. The austere ending is in keeping with her idea of *death so slowly approaching, which makes us see the things of this life with very different eyes from those through which we see them in health.* She had felt this herself since the summer of 1677, and, as Mme. de Sévigné indicates, had composed her soul for the end. The extinction of all her illusions is displayed in the shrinking fear she makes Mme. de Clèves express, that marriage may be the tomb of the prince's love, and the beginning of jealousies: it is this dread, indeed, as much as any scruple about duty, which operates in the mind of Mme. de Clèves, in opposition to the idea of marriage with her lover. In perfecting their ideal romance, it is evident that the two friends, M. de la Rochefoucauld and Mme. de la Fayette, in questioning the supposed felicity of their hero and heroine, still considered their own calmly affectionate connection as the most secure and comfortable.

They did not enjoy it much longer. In the night between the 16th and 17th of March, two years that very day after the publication of the *Princesse de Clèves*, M. de la Rochefoucauld died. "My head is so full of this misfortune and of the extreme affliction of our poor friend," writes Mme. de Sévigné, "that I must speak of it to you. . . . M. de Marsallac is indescribably afflicted; however, my child, he will console himself with the King and the court; all his children will find some one to take his place; but where will Mme. de la Fayette find such a friend again, such companionship, such gentleness, such pleasantness, such confidence, such consideration for her and for her son? She is infirm, confined to her room, unable to go about. M. de la Rochefoucauld was also sedentary; this made them necessary to each other, and nothing could equal the confidence and charm of their friendship. Think of it, my child; you will find it scarcely possible that there could be a greater loss, one which time could do less to repair. I have not left my poor friend all these days; she could not join the crowding family, she needed some one to have pity on her. Mme. de Coulanges has done very well also, and we shall remain some time yet." And in every letter which followed: "Poor Mme. de la Fayette does not know what to do with herself. . . . They are all consoled excepting her." This is what Mme. de Sévigné repeats over and over again, and every time more expressively than before: "This poor creature, do what she will, cannot fill that vacant place." Mme. de la Fayette did not seek to fill it up; she knew that such losses cannot be replaced. Even that tender friendship with Mme. de Sévigné was not enough, she knew that well; there was too much to divide them. To convince oneself of the incompleteness of such friendships, even the greatest and dearest, we have but to read Mme. de la Fayette's letter to Mme. de Sévigné on the 8th of

October 1689, so matchless, so peremptory, and so urgently unceremonious in its affection, and afterwards to read the commentary Mme. de Sévigné makes on it in writing to her daughter,—"Good gracious! what a fine proposition, to have no more a house of my own, to be dependent, to have no equipage, and to owe a thousand *écus!*"—and we will understand that it does not do to expect everything from such friendships unless they are quite undivided, since even the most delicate can judge thus. After love, after absolute friendship with no reservation or thought for any other besides, there is only death or God.

Mme. de la Fayette lived thirteen years longer: we have Mme. de Sévigné to refer to for some slender details regarding her outward life during these lonely years. A hastily formed intimacy with the young Mme. de Schomberg awakened the curiosity and the jealousy of older friends; it does not appear that this effort of a heart which had found something to cling to was an enduring effort. It was probably the same restless yearning which, in the early months of her loss, led her to again enlarge her already vast rooms from the garden side, even as, alas! her life was waning. She also seems to have filled up her time by writing some things which are now lost. *La Comtesse de Tende* must have been written during these years.

Bussy's most severe criticism, and also that of the world at large, on the subject of *La Princesse de Clèves*, was called forth by the extraordinary confession which the heroine makes to her husband; Mme. de la Fayette, in inventing another similar situation, which led to a still more extraordinary confession, thought that the first would thus be so far justified. She succeeded in *La Comtesse de Tende*, although greater art was neces-

sary to give the *Princesse de Clèves* a sister worthy of
her: we feel that the author has a limit, and is drawing
near it.

Les Mémoires de la Cour de France, for the years
1688 and 1689, are remarkable for sequence, precision,
and freedom from prejudice; no wandering from the
point, scarcely any reflections, even; a vivid, impressive
narrative, always intelligent. The author of such a
work was certainly capable of more important things. I
have quoted her cutting remark on Mme. de Maintenon
à *propos* of *Esther*. Racine, therefore, and his *Comedie
de Couvent* is treated rather slightingly: "Mme. de
Maintenon, to amuse her little girls and the King,
ordered a comedy to be written by Racine, the best
poet of the day, who was taken from his poetry, in
which he is inimitable, to make of it, to his own misfortune, and that of all who can appreciate good plays,
a very imitable historian." Mme. de la Fayette's circle
preferred Corneille to Racine. In *Zayde*, she had
imitated that Spanish style so dear to the author of
the *Cid*, and which Racine and Boileau had super-
seded. She often saw Fontenelle, and her particular
friends were men like Segrais and Huet, who both disliked, almost hated, those two reigning poets, Racine
and Boileau. M. de la Rochefoucauld, who admired
them both as writers, found that they possessed only
one kind of talent, and considered them poor company
outside their poetry. Lastly, Valincour, who had
attacked the *Princesse de Clèves*, was the pupil and
intimate friend of both. But Mme. de la Fayette was
too talented and too just not to admire as they deserved, authors whose tenderness and justice found in
her such ready chords of harmony. At the moment
when her reverence for Racine was at its lowest, she
calls him *the best poet, and inimitable*. We have seen

that at Gourville's house, in which she was almost at home, *La poétique* of Boileau was read before her. We have observed how many qualities she possessed in common with Despréaux,* upright judgment, incontestable criticism ; also, in her way, she was an oracle of wisdom to her circle. Numerous expressions of hers have been retained which are exactly in Boileau's style ; we add the following to those of them we have already quoted : "He who sets himself above others, however great his talent, puts himself below that talent." Boileau, in conversation with D'Olivet, one day said, "Do you know why the ancients had so few admirers? Because at least three-fourths of those who have translated them have been either ignorant persons or fools. Mme. de la Fayette, the woman in France who possessed the greatest talent, and who wrote best, compared a stupid translator to a servant who is sent by his mistress to deliver a compliment to some one. What his mistress has told him in polite language to say, he goes and expresses clumsily, he maims the message ; the more delicacy there is in the compliment, the less able is the servant to convey its meaning. This, in few words, is the most perfect image of a bad translator." Boileau, therefore, seems himself to certify the fact of this resemblance, this affinity which we have indicated.

M. Rœderer is quite right with regard to Molière's relations with the circle formed by Mmes. de Sévigné and de la Fayette, when he declares that the *femmes savantes* had no reference to them at all. As for La Fontaine, it is well known that at one time he was on intimate terms with Mme. de la Fayette ; we have his very friendly lines addressed to her when

* Boileau.—Tr.

sending her a little billiard-table, about the same time that he dedicated a fable to the author of the *Maximes*, and another to Mlle. de Sévigné.*

After M. de la Rochefoucauld's death, Mme. de la Fayette's thoughts became more strongly fixed on religious subjects; we have trustworthy evidence of this in a long and beautiful letter from Du Guet to her. She had chosen him as her director. Without being absolutely connected with Port-Royal, all her inclinations lay in that direction, and the hypocrisy of the court also influenced this tendency. We have seen that her stepfather was the *Chevalier Renaud de Sévigné*, uncle of Mme. de Sévigné, and one of the benefactors of Port-Royal-des-Champs, the cloister of which he

---

* Mme. de la Fayette was therefore actually of the same group, the same Parnassus, so to speak, as La Fontaine, Racine, and Despréaux;[1] and the following little story is simply a rather childish version of the truth: "In 1675," we are told by Ménage, "Mme. de Thianges gave to M. le Duc du Maine, as a New Year's gift, a gilded room about the siz   table. Over the door was written in large letters, *Chambre du Sublime*. In the room was a bed with a *balustre*,[2] and a large easy-chair, in which sat M. le Duc du Maine, made in wax, a very good likeness. Near him stood M. de la Rochefoucauld, to whom he was handing some verses to examine. Standing round, were M. de Marsillac and M. Bossuet, then Bishop of Condom. In a corner of the alcove were Mme. de Thianges and Mme. de la Fayette, reading some verses. Outside the *balustre*, Despréaux, with a pitchfork, was preventing seven or eight wretched poets from entering. Racine was near Despréaux, and a little farther off La Fontaine, to whom he was making a sign to come forward. All these figures were of wax and in miniature, and each person represented had given his own." Ménage does not inform us if he himself posed as one of the wretched poets driven away by Boileau.

---

[1] Boileau.—TR.   [2] A railed-off recess.—TR.

had rebuilt. He did not die till 1672.* Mme. de la Fayette knew Du Guet, who had begun to exercise great influence on the spiritual direction of consciences, and who, in the decline of Port-Royal, held only to its righteous traditions, avoiding all shallow contentiousness. Here are some of the earnest words which this spiritually-minded priest addressed to the penitent who had requested them from him:—

"I have considered, Madame, that you ought to employ usefully the earliest moments of the day in which you cease to sleep only to begin to dream. I know your thoughts are not then connected thoughts, and that very often your chief endeavour is to have no thoughts, and it is difficult not to yield to this inclination when one would willingly let it rule; it is easier to give way than to overcome self. It is therefore important that you should nourish yourself on more solid food than aimless thoughts, the most innocent of which are useless; and I believe you could not better employ such a peaceful time than in taking thought to yourself of a life already very long, and of which there remains to you now only a reputation the vanity of which you yourself understand better than any one. Till now the

---

* Towards the last, Mme. de la Fayette's relations with Port-Royal were more direct than I had thought. I read in a letter from Racine to M. de Bonrepaux (28th July 1693): "Your friend Mme. de la Fayette gave us very melancholy entertainment. I had not been fortunate enough to see her during the latter years of her life. God had cast a salutary shadow over all her worldly occupations, and she died, after suffering in solitude and admirable resignation from her severe infirmities, receiving great support from the ministrations of M. l'Abbé Du Guet and some of the *Messieurs* of Port-Royal, whom she held in great veneration, and this caused Mme. la Comtesse de Grammont to praise them very highly, for she openly holds Port-Royal in high esteem."

clouds with which you have tried to envelop religion have deceived even you yourself. As it is by its aid alone that one can and ought to examine and know oneself, in affecting to ignore it you have only ignored yourself. It is time to put everything in its place, and to put yourself in yours. Truth will be your judge, and you are here but to follow that and not to be the judge of it. In vain we defend ourselves, in vain we deceive: the veil is rent asunder as life and its inordinate desires fade away; and we are convinced that we shall lead an altogether new life when we are no longer permitted to dwell here. We must therefore begin by an earnest desire to see ourselves as we are seen by our Judge. Such self-knowledge is grievous even for such as have been least self-deceived. It divests us of all our virtues, even of our good qualities, and of all the esteem they have acquired for us. We feel that till then we have been living in falsehood and delusion; that we have been feeding on painted food; that we have used virtue only as a cloak, and neglected to search our hearts, because that searching means trusting all to God and to salvation, despising oneself in all things, not through a wiser kind of vanity, a more enlightened, more cultivated pride, but because we are convinced of our wrong-doing and wretchedness."

The remainder of the letter is equally admirable, and in this urgent and appropriate tone: "Thus you who have dreamed, cease your dreams! You who have been esteemed *sincere* above others, and on whom the world has bestowed this flattery, you are not so; you have never been more than half sincere; without God, your wisdom was but a cultivated mind." Further on I read a sentence on those years "when one has not yet sincerely repented, because one is minded to excuse one's weakness, and *to love what has caused it.*" *

A year before her death, Mme. de la Fayette wrote to Mme. de Sévigné a short note, in which she describes her miserable condition, unable to sleep either by night or by day, her resignation to God's will; and she ends in these words: "Believe, my dear friend, that I have loved you better than any other human being." That other affection which she no more named, no longer took into account, was it at last expunged, consumed away in sacrifice?

There is harmony to the very last, and now it ends. Mme. de Sévigné writes to Mme. de Guitaud on the 3rd June 1693, two or three days after the fatal day, deploring the death of that faithful friend of forty years: ". . . For two years her infirmity had been extreme; I always defended her against those who said she was foolish not to go out. 'She is sad unto death,' I used to tell them: still they would insist, saying, 'What folly! is she not the most fortunate woman in the world?' Those persons were very hasty in their censure, and I only replied, 'Mme. de la Fayette is not foolish,' and I adhered to this. Alas! Madame, the poor creature is now justified. . . . She had heart disease. Was this not enough to account for her paroxysms of pain? She was right in her life, and she is right after death; and she was never without that *divine raison* which was her chief characteristic. She remained unconscious during the four days of her last illness. For our consolation, God granted us a special favour, a distinct sign of her predestination; namely, that she confessed on the festival of *Corpus Christi* with

* In his youth, Du Guet had tried to write a sentimental romance, and he greatly admired *L'Astrée;* he was a most suitable director for the author of *La Princesse de Clèves.*

an accuracy and sincerity which could have come only from God, and received the holy sacrament in the same spirit. Thus, my dear Madame, we regard the communion which she was accustomed to make at Whitsuntide as God's merciful kindness to console us that she was not in a state to receive the viaticum."

Thus died and lived in an atmosphere of gentle sadness, painful suffering, worldly wisdom, and Christian repentance, she whose ideal production enchants us. What more can we add either for reflection or instruction? Do not the letter to Mme. de Sablé, *La Princesse de Clèves*, and the letter of Du Guet, contain the whole story of a life?

www.ingramcontent.com/pod-product-compliance
Lightning Source LLC
Chambersburg PA
CBHW031816230426
43669CB00009B/1160